NO DUMBING DOWN

D1235829

A No-nonsense Guide for
CEOs on Organization Growth

Karen D. Walker

BUSINESS EXPERT PRESS

No Dumbing Down™: A No-nonsense Guide for CEOs on Organization Growth
Copyright © Business Expert Press, LLC, 2018.

All rights reserved. No part of this publication may be reproduced, stored in a retrieval system, or transmitted in any form or by any means—electronic, mechanical, photocopy, recording, or any other—except for brief quotations, not to exceed 250 words, without the prior permission of the publisher.

First published in 2018 by
Business Expert Press, LLC
222 East 46th Street, New York, NY 10017
www.businessexpertpress.com

ISBN-13: 978-1-94744-180-4 (paperback)
ISBN-13: 978-1-94744-181-1 (e-book)

Business Expert Press Human Resource Management and Organizational Behavior Collection

Collection ISSN: 1946-5637 (print)
Collection ISSN: 1946-5645 (electronic)

Cover and interior design by S4Carlisle Publishing Services Private Ltd., Chennai, India

First edition: 2018

10 9 8 7 6 5 4 3 2 1

Printed in the United States of America.

Abstract

No Dumbing Down™: A No-nonsense Guide for CEOs on Organization Growth is a book for a company's executive leaders looking to make improvements when aligning the organization's internal and external strategies for fast, profitable, and sustainable growth. Learn how to do the one job only you can do: aligning the organization's internal and external strategies for fast, profitable, and sustainable growth. As one of the first employees at Compaq Computers, Karen Walker was part of the senior team that grew the company's revenue from zero to $111 million in its first year. By the time she decided to leave 14 years later, Compaq had grown to $15 billion. Needless to say, it was a formative experience for Karen, and today, as a consultant, the Compaq work has provided her with the exact tools needed to help leaders. Karen's consulting business delves into every imaginable market where she assists leaders to master the counterintuitive art of organizational growth and success. Helping everyone from Fortune 500s to start-ups deliver on the promise that they've made to their customers, her motto is truly "no dumbing down." This book will serve as the perfect instruction manual for growing your business beyond what you thought was possible.

Keywords

business, CEO, C-suite, executive, growth, innovation, leaders, leadership, management, organization, scale up, startup, venture capital

Contents

Foreword

by Rod Canion
Founder and former CEO, Compaq Computer Corporation

Author of *Open*

Only Karen Walker could write a book entitled *No Dumbing Down*—phrasing like that couldn't be closer to what she is about and who she is.

With her background in industrial engineering, Karen has a keen understanding of systems and what it takes to make them work. She's leveraged these experiences to become an excellent model for all kinds of leaders, including organization executives who go on to become consultants. Her work with people like me—CEOs and other senior leaders in growth-oriented organizations—generates results because of her unusual, yet, formidable mixture of business acumen with her intolerance for corporate politics. She knows when and where to take a stand and turn inactivity into action.

When we founded Compaq, one of our primary goals was to create a *good place to work*. That goal encompassed both *what* we did as well as *how* we did it. Our company's work ethic was not only efficient and effective, but it was also immensely rewarding for so many people. As the company grew, so did we. Karen was one of the many to walk away having learned extremely valuable lessons. But what I find most remarkable is how she's been able to transpose these experiences so brilliantly into her consulting work today.

At each juncture of this book, she will show you how to support growth in your organization in proven and insightful ways. She will also make it clear why only *you* can make it happen. The five core principles she outlines, coupled with a compatible product/market fit, were critical to Compaq's incredible growth, and I believe they have been key to the expansion of many other successful companies. An organization that lacks these principles—even with an excellent product/market fit—will begin to decline over time. Her approach, focusing on the internal strategies to support growth, is indispensable.

When it comes to running a business, none of us has time for approaches that leave us asking, "So what?" In our decade of working together, Karen demonstrated an unflappable bias for action and an obsession for meaningful results. Her book will enable you to achieve those same kinds of results and all the different types of success that goes with them.

Preface

No Dumbing Down™: *A No-nonsense Guide for CEOs on Organization Growth* is a book for a company's senior-most leaders. It teaches you how to do a job only you can do: aligning the organization's internal and external strategies for profitable, sustainable growth.

Why do leaders need this guidance? The problem is that too often, corporate leaders misunderstand what it takes to grow.

When most companies try to grow, they invariably emphasize on sales and increasing revenue at the expense of making sure they've aligned the infrastructure needed to support that expansion. The result?

Sales outpace the firm's ability to fulfill its promises.

Suddenly, product quality drops; employees get overwhelmed by rework; missing commitments produces dissatisfied customers; firefighting becomes the norm; top people run for the exits; and the reputation of the business tanks.

What happened? It's not that Marketing forecast demand poorly, or that Sales couldn't close, or that Engineering designed a lousy product. It's that the organization was missing cross-functional alignment.

Only senior leaders can fix this. They are the ones who have the necessary control, they can see from above. They can make sure that what happens *inside* the company can support what's happening *outside.*

This book will help CEOs and other senior leaders create and align the internal strategies and structures that support external growth. That's because early in my career, I got hooked on growth: fast, powerful business growth.

Years ago, I was one of the first employees at Compaq Computer, when it was the fastest growing company in American history. As employee #104, I was part of the senior team that increased the company's revenues in its first year from zero to $111 million. Five years later, Compaq hit the $1 billion revenue mark, taking the least amount of time (contemporaneously) to reach that milestone. You can imagine the exhilaration and stress of that growth curve! By the time, I decided to leave 14 years later, Compaq had grown nearly 15,000 times bigger, to $15 billion.

What I've done for the past couple of decades in my consulting practice, and what I do today, is to help companies—from start-ups to Fortune 500 firms—grow fast, profitably and sustainably. I've taken what I learned at Compaq and applied it over and over again, in the process identifying which strategies deliver long-lasting results most quickly.

Those strategies work because they take direct aim at pitfalls that can trip up even the most stellar companies, such as:

- Teams that don't work to their full potential because internal forces cause them to dumb down their output.
- Processes, tools, and behaviors that are stuck in the status quo, lacking the agility and responsiveness to keep up with change.
- People's inability to handle unexpected events and to prevent the company from careening off in directions that undermine critical strategies.
- An emphasis on the short term and the urgent, at the expense of the long view, and the nurturing of scalable, replicable success.

This book shows senior leaders how to—and why to—capitalize on five proven strategies for aligning the skills and efforts of top management. I've chosen these five because they are most impactful. Any others can't match the speed and results of the five presented here.

Overall, this work will make an organization more agile. And "agile" is a word chosen with care. As used by software developers, it denotes a process that enables rapid response to fast-breaking, fast-changing customer requests. This book takes the intention of that process and applies it to the dynamic environments and other challenges most companies face every day. The solutions mapped out are all about improving collaboration, co-creation, and flexibility and providing outstanding value throughout the process.

A CEO can't sit down with his or her market and say, "Tell me what you want, and every two weeks I'll adjust accordingly." Companies can search for trends, talk with individual customers, and even try to force change, but they still can't predict the outcomes, nor direct them in their favor. This book reveals how top managers can and must develop new abilities to be responsive, to get entire organizations aligned for responsiveness, and to enhance profitability over the long term.

Acknowledgments

This book is, in many ways, a distillation of my life and learning—so far. I'm grateful to many people for helping me arrive at this place where my talent, passion, and the market all intersect.

First and foremost, I send my gratitude to my clients. Without you, there is no impetus for growth. I've been greatly influenced by our partnerships. A special word of thanks to: Kathy Miller, Dave Keil, Dave Gould, Ed Murray, Mike Sullivan, Steve Schlesinger, and Dave Finney, among many others.

Thank you to my colleagues, mentors, and advisors: Mark Levy, Gabe Kahan, Alan Weiss, Dorie Clark, and to the many Lisas in my life.

Heartfelt thanks to Rod Canion and my colleagues from Compaq Computer, who showed me what was possible with no dumbing down.

Finally, I want to thank my husband, Dr. Bob, who is fond of saying that he taught me everything he knew. I hope I've proven to be a good student.

Growth Is Not Just About Increasing Sales Revenue

CHAPTER 1

Introduction

Are You Doing Your Best Work?

Enthusiasm is the mother of effort, and without it, nothing great was ever achieved.

—Ralph Waldo Emerson

At 25, I gave my notice and walked away from a stable, well-paying job. What was I thinking?

It was 1982, and I was working as a branch manager for Texas Instruments. After four years and a series of promotions, I was comfortable in my role as a female director in a male-dominated industry. We were working on commercial digital hardware using silicon transistors and integrated circuits. I received a promotion every 6 months. As an industrial engineer, it was an ideal situation. But, I began to notice a shift in the company.

Several well-regarded managers were leaving the business. Word got around that there was a new venture starting by the name of "Gateway." Without warning, I saw a number of my firm's brightest and most driven colleagues leave their jobs for the new enterprise. These were all people I admired a great deal.

And it didn't stop. So many people left their jobs at Texas Instruments that the company filed a lawsuit against the new venture for poaching its employees. The tension was rising. What could drive my colleagues to give up their job security at Texas Instruments?

It was time to investigate.

Everyone leaving had been involved with the business of manufacturing hard drives, so we all assumed the new company focused on electronics—we made lots of guesses, but no one knew. Whatever it was, the management of the new business couldn't let me in on the secret because of the lawsuit. But while their mouths remained shut, their arms opened wide.

Without disclosing what I'd be doing, the new venture welcomed me onto the team. "I don't think I can do this job," I told the hiring managers, unsure if my qualifications would be adequate. They smiled, shook their heads, assured me that I could handle it, and ushered me into my new future. Little did I know the venture I had just joined would go on to become Compaq Computer—a corporation that would set a new precedent as the fastest growing company America had ever seen. (You might ask, what happened to the name Gateway? They changed their name to Compaq just prior to launching the first product.)

Yet my decision to join the new venture wasn't tied to any technological innovation. Because no products had been launched, I assumed I would now be spending my days supporting the design and manufacture of hard drives. But this wasn't the deciding factor. I decided I wanted a piece of the action because of the *people* who were joining the new firm.

In addition to pioneering the portable computer, the company was founded with the goal of creating a business environment that offered a wonderful place to work in. Our products were only one variable in the equation. There was vibrancy in our day-to-day operations that transcended any professional team to which I had previously belonged. Everyone who came to work wanted to be there, and it showed.

Garnering massive growth in our first year—over $100 million in sales—we became an indomitable team of intrapreneurs. We collaborated on everything, running into every imaginable problem, and tackling each one with the same eagerness and fortitude. There was an explicit awareness of cause and effect. The impact of every individual contribution, or lack thereof, was felt by all.

While this high-performing environment combined with an enviable product/market opportunity allowed the company to expand rapidly, it also encouraged its workers to grow in parallel. I was able to push myself further than ever before with my new found autonomy. I learned that solving technical problems was not difficult. In reality, building healthy interpersonal relations was more challenging, and it took work. This came as a surprise—nothing in my past had prepared me for the realization that *how people worked* mattered as much as *what they did*. Not only that, but I learned that to be a true superstar as a leader, you had to excel in both areas: solving technical problems and leading people with compassion and understanding.

About 14 years later, the company had achieved monolithic proportions. We'd grown to 17,000 employees worldwide and grossed $15 billion in annual revenue. But something had changed.

We had begun to hire people who were joining the company for little more than our benefits. At first, we settled for this only occasionally when the need to fill a seat was overwhelming. But it began to occur more and more frequently. The people coming on board weren't bad people, just motivated to achieve different goals than those of our original team.

This difference in personnel diluted the single-minded passion and drive we once enjoyed. An old professional dynamic began to show its face; office politics grew rampant. Taking stock of the climate, I decided it was time to leave.

I got my next job consulting for a company in San Francisco. Inexperienced, yet ambitious, I flew out to the Bay Area and, shortly, thereafter, met my husband. We partnered to form Oneteam Consulting, the firm I now lead. Fast forward 20 years, and here I am writing a book about what I've learned while advising CEOs and their senior leadership teams on how to uncover their organization's potential.

But those two decades were crucial. I encountered organizations struggling with inconsistencies in leadership, operations, workplace culture, and every other facet of a business. And while each of my clients dealt with constricted growth in unique circumstances, the fundamental roadblock was always the same.

Every one of these organizations was experiencing misaligned *internal* and *external strategies*.

By this, I mean that what was happening *within* the company was affecting its overall growth. Its level of performance was being unintentionally *dumbed down*. Sounds obvious, right? The issues themselves were never devilishly complex—recognizing them was half the battle.

Here are a couple of telling examples.

Imagine an organization focused on increased sales. They're directing all their attention and resources toward their customer base, and their marketing department is finding explosive success in gaining people's attention. But what happens when they bite off more than they can chew?

Their external strategy may involve gathering a large pool of sales, but internally, they may not have the workforce or systems to deliver on their promises. Now they run the risk of disappointing customers and losing future sales, a move that may be fatal. It's this discrepancy between what they've agreed to on the outside versus what they're capable of on the inside that will impede progress.

Next, picture an organization that is reactive. One quarter they're focused on propping up sales, next they're focused on hiring, and next, they concentrate on ramping up their marketing. Their internal processes allow no room for juggling all of the different activities a successful business needs to survive. This dysfunction creates a haphazard and lopsided external strategy. They constantly have one department outpacing the others. As a result, their customers begin experiencing the organization as unreliable.

There is no substitute for a solid fit between product and market. But understand here that a superior product/market fit isn't enough. If an organization's internal operations prevent it from operating successfully, it won't matter how brilliant its product or business model may be. A dumbed-down input ensures a dumbed-down output.

Now, let's take a look at the big picture. Managing a company amidst evolving industries, innovative competitors, and unprecedented customer demands can cause enough worry. But many business leaders fail to understand that misaligned internal and external strategies create additional problems for them and the organization they lead. A CEO can wind up shooting himself (or herself) in the foot—scrambling to react to issues he (or she) could have, and should have, foreseen.

I often describe my work as "helping businesses realize their potential." As you look to the future, it's always best to optimize your current operations. Not only does this reinforce the strengths you already have, but it also allows for bigger and better long-term rewards.

A useful metaphor for this occurs in real estate. As a developer, your goal is to create the *highest and best use* of the property on which you work. You want to optimize every element of design you can to appease regulations, while ensuring your investment is as profitable as possible.

Similarly, what is your organization's potential? You want to optimize your productivity, profitability, and feasibility. You want to make sure that they are aligned with you and those with whom you're working. What's more, you want to make success sustainable.

It's important to understand that the strategies I reveal here have less to do with *creating* growth, and more to do with *supporting* growth. An organization's success will always come from its product/market fit, or how successfully it is serving its market. What I'm offering, however, are methodologies for unearthing your capabilities and minimizing your blind spots, allowing you to serve your market in an improved way.

What do you see when all these stars are aligned? Cohesive teamwork. Enthusiastic workers. Explicit communication. Collaborative decision making. A bias for the right actions at the right times. Your whole organization should be functioning as a high-performance unit.

These group dynamics were fundamental to my time at Compaq. I will never forget the experience of working in such an exciting and high-energy environment. Many of you reading this have experienced this yourself, and most of us have tried to duplicate it again and again. It's hard, I know. But I can show you how to get there.

And this goes for organizations at all levels of success. While I believe there's always room to refine strategies, this book doesn't serve only companies that are struggling. These strategies apply to a whole spectrum of circumstances.

Maybe you feel you're already operating at full capacity. Perhaps your organization is doing well, but you know it can do better. What if your board says you've had a great year, but there's room for improvement and you're not quite sure how to get there? Maybe your organization is outpacing its capacity. Or perhaps new people have joined the leadership team. Times of transition can always greatly benefit from closely aligned strategies. If you find yourself in any of these situations, this is a perfect time to assess your internal and external alignment in order to avoid any fatal mistakes.

Why stunt your growth with below-average performance? Eradicate any dumbed-down strategies to lead your organization to its full potential.

CHAPTER 2

For Senior Leaders Only

Interdependence is and ought to be as much the ideal of man as self-sufficiency. Man is a social being.

—Mahatma Gandhi

So I've told you the *what* and *why.* Now let me cover the *who.* Who will this book serve? Why them and not others?

This piece of the puzzle is critical to generating real change. My strategies for optimized performance may be useful to a variety of workers situated within an organization, but they will only gain widespread adoption if a select few spearhead them.

This distinctive power is in the hands of the senior leaders and the CEO.

Before I explain why, I want to emphasize that while a CEO is the paramount authority of any organization, he or she is not always best suited for remedying dumbed-down operations.

Because the CEO is the liaison between the board of directors and the rest of the organization, he or she is typically faced with making impactful decisions every day. Coordinating the work of thousands of employees and directing the fate of an organization demand a macroscopic approach that often leaves little room for the kinds of tactical, hands-on support that is the responsibility of the senior leadership team.

Of course, you typically have only *one* CEO, but have a senior leadership *team.* Senior leaders can work together, allowing each team member to supervise and support one another. This provides them with an advantage.

Why exactly are senior leaders such potent catalysts for change? The first reason should be obvious—their seniority allows for a wide-ranging, aerial view of their organization. Their jobs revolve around measuring the success of entire departments, rather than smaller subsections.

Because they operate as a group, senior leaders can observe their particular divisions in relation to one another. Each senior leader's vantage point can be cross-operational, requiring cross-organizational cooperation from the other leaders. Aligning internal and external strategies can only be done holistically; otherwise, you wind up with one department outperforming the others. Spearheading this kind of transformation is where the senior leadership team shines.

Next, senior leaders approach their jobs with a long-term perspective. While an organization rewards most workers for short-term results, senior leaders are preoccupied with ensuring success over much longer periods of time. Never mind this week or this month—they're typically worried about this year, or the next 5 years.

Likewise, their goals are much broader. "How do we double our revenue in 2 years? How do we scale to 10,000 employees by this year? How do we improve customer satisfaction with as little expense as possible?" They want to be able to document their progress with precision.

Finally, senior leaders are essential for aligning internal and external strategies because of their unique ability to hold the organization, as a whole, accountable. Given that each leader's success is inherently tied to the success of their peers, as well as the success of their subordinates, there are several levels of accountability at play.

To start off, each senior leader is, of course, the primary supervisor of strategy and execution among his or her team. Senior leaders are updated on the status of projects and general operations. Reports get circulated, dashboards are monitored, and plans are continually being analyzed and revised—to ensure the results leaders are seeking.

At the same time, they are also being held mutually accountable. Because senior leaders are experienced in setting and meeting goals, it's often easy for them to keep themselves and the rest of their team in check.

Those who don't excel in these ways get replaced rather quickly. Consider a team where some leaders are high-performing and accountable, but others aren't. Any efficiency disintegrates. Because certain departments become undependable, the high-performing leaders are thrown off kilter because their success is tied to the organization functioning as a whole. The success of every senior leader is dependent upon that of the other team members. Each senior leader must be clear about what they need from all other senior leaders, as well as vice versa.

Achieving this synergy is, of course, not always a walk in the park. But that's why you're reading this book. After two decades in the field, I've devised five core strategies for aligning internal and external operations. As a consultant, my clients have ranged from small startups to large international corporations. These strategies are all-encompassing and meant for businesses of all shapes and sizes.

Each strategy confronts misaligned internal and external processes from a different angle. Put together, they are a surefire way to support all potential for long-term and sustainable growth.

But I will warn you. Nowhere in here will I attempt to tackle the specifics of every imaginable obstacle you can encounter. Instead, my focus will be to inform and empower you—the senior leader.

Be it the granule of sales percentages or the overarching importance of communicating your agenda to your peers, your attention must be on high-performance teams and interpersonal relationships. As I said in the last chapter, technical problems are rarely the showstopper, but interpersonal problems have the potential to cripple an organization if they are not well managed.

This was where Compaq reigned supreme. With the right intentions, strategy, and teamwork, your organization can succeed too.

SECTION 2

The Five Internal Strategies

CHAPTER 3

No Dumbing Down

How "Teamwork-as-Usual" Hurts Your Organization and What to Do about It

Alone we can do so little; together we can do so much.

—Helen Keller

We've all experienced it. It's one of the biggest reasons why an organization's internal and external strategies misalign and misfire. It's why some of your highest performing people find their work to be disconnected from their talents.

It's teamwork-as-usual.

It typically kicks off at an all-hands company meeting. A facilitator often leads the group, putting everyone through a series of physical activities meant to simulate what it's like to work well together. Trust falls and the like.

Attendees receive t-shirts, hats, and mugs. The boss enthusiastically calls for everyone to go forth and work as one. Expectations are high. People leave thinking, "Maybe this time we *can* get things done together." And everyone tries—really tries.

At first, teamwork seems to improve, with flashes of the cross-functional potential that is the promise of every team. But then old, unproductive patterns reemerge. Office politics come into play. Conflicts arise and aren't managed. People delay making decisions. Soon, employees stop talking, taking risks, and sharing information. Expectations fall, and internal–external misalignments appear.

Managers may try to fix things by making every decision a team collaboration, but find that holding meetings eats up so much time that progress grinds to a halt. Or they recognize that their priorities and resources are misaligned, and don't know how to correct the problem.

Eventually, high performers get fed up. The team appears to be a tar pit. For all their talents, employees lack the skills to work together in a group setting. And the team manager doesn't have the skills to lead them. It's teamwork-as-usual, but with a dumbed-down output.

Dumbing down is insidious, like a corporate virus. It gets a foothold on the day when you decide it's not worth pushing your team to do the right thing. Maybe there's so much on your plate that you promote compromise just so that the group—and you—can move on. Or you keep quiet when someone is rebuked for putting forward an idea that, although sensible, didn't fit the prevailing corporate politics. Or you see misaligned priorities, but don't try to correct them.

Here are good, even brilliant, people trying their best to work effectively. But they cave in to mediocrity. Why do these messes occur?

A team can only function at the level of its lowest performing member. It's like a chain. If one link is weak, it doesn't matter how strong the others are. They'll all be useless if one snaps.

I've recently taken up the sport of rowing, which offers some useful analogies. I used to imagine rowing as an intensive arm and back exercise, but quickly learned it's about the legs. If your arms are strong, but your legs are weak, you might start off quickly and vigorously, but you'll eventually slow down to the pace your legs can handle.

The same thing applies to teams. If you have one weak team member, you might be able to carry him for a short while. If you have more than one, forget it—even the highest performing tire of the extra effort that is required. One by one their contributions diminish. Soon, the boat flounders or sinks in the water.

I frequently find new clients with organizations that are financially successful and filled with hardworking people, but with vast potential being left out on the conference room table.

I see people working at cross-purposes, their "schedule versus cost" priorities misaligned. And often these conflicts are only resolved by the loudest voice in the room, not the smartest.

I watch project kickoff meetings that are exciting and full of hope. But then "reality" sets in. Enthusiasm tempers. And excitement about the work fades into an attitude of "just getting by." The workers have, subconsciously, dumbed down their operations. And they're not alone. It happens all the time, almost everywhere.

I often ask leaders in these organizations about their past experiences on teams—to describe their best and worst team experiences. It's critical for the leaders to think about this and answer it themselves. Their responses are the same nine times out of 10.

Here's what they say about the worst teams—the ones that dumb down (Figure 3.1).

Are you nodding your head in agreement? These worst behaviors are forces that oppose high performance. Some are obvious, but others are less so. And any one of these can prevent people from doing their best work.

Figure 3.1 Behaviors of worst teams

This scenario occurs, time after time, in company after company. We continue paying attention to the idea of teamwork and all its trappings ("Don't forget to order the t-shirts!"). But we don't attend to what it takes for a team actually to work.

It is, after all, called *team*work. Not individuals-gathered-in-a-room work. It is based on how we interact with one another in a group. We think this happens automatically and so we don't address it; and dumbing down occurs.

After decades of working with hundreds of teams, I know that most people want to do good work. They want to do something that they are proud of, that's respected, and that makes a difference. They don't come into your organization intending to dumb down.

So what goes wrong?

There are three primary causes of dumbing down.

1. **Blind spots**

    Often, we don't see that dumbing down is happening. But then one day, you have an experience where you *do* get to work at full potential, and you realize what you've been missing.

    It's like the old story of the frog in a pot of water. Content at first, the frog doesn't sense the water's heating up until it's too late.

    My time at Compaq is a perfect example.

    The company started with a small group of employees who were fervent about the idea of a new product and—*something equally important*—the company was also a great place to work. But as I explained in Chapter 1, the vibrancy of our environment began to decline. Our hires began to flood through the door—hardworking, yet not fully invested in the business.

    The influx of new people diluted the passion and drive we once enjoyed. Office politics crept back into the environment. Strategic alignments went askew. And even worse, we were blind to what was happening.

    But others saw it. An outside vendor told me later, "Before, people were always in the building working. There was a steady hum, a glow. After the change, I'd see people streaming out the door at 5:00. The entire feeling of the place, at all times, was different."

Compaq went on to have a few more successful years, but was ultimately subsumed by Hewlett-Packard.

2. **Over-applied individualism**

Teamwork is a concept to which most people haven't paid attention. We aren't born knowing how to master it. It's something we have to learn.

Usually, though, we assume that the skill set for working as an individual will serve us similarly as a team member. Though the skills needed for each situation are similar, they're not carbon copies. Nevertheless, we use the same formulas that made us successful as *individuals* to solving the problems of *teams*.

Many of the best teams are sports teams. In sports, it's very obvious who's playing at his potential and who's not. You can see the problems right away. If a basketball player has a bad game, the coach can call a timeout and implement a correction.

Remember the worst teams exercise? Look at this list of typical behaviors seen in the best teams (Figure 3.2).

Individual contributors, usually chosen for their technical skills alone, rarely possess the skills to demonstrate these behaviors. This oversight is a force that can diminish an organization's potential.

3. **Cultural constraints**

In my consulting practice, I was once called into a Boston tech company by a former client with a new Senior Vice President (SVP) role. He gave me an overview of the organization—not only the potential that attracted him to the company, but also the cultural malaise he experienced after arriving. Next, he introduced me to his new Chief Executive Officer (CEO).

As the two of us sat, one-on-one in his office, the CEO began to tell me what a horrible place this was to work. He described a leadership team and organization in the throes of dumbing down.

But then, as we talked, he had his "aha moment." The revelatory moment consultants live for when the root problem suddenly becomes obvious to the client.

Remember the
BEST/WORST TEAM EXERCISE?

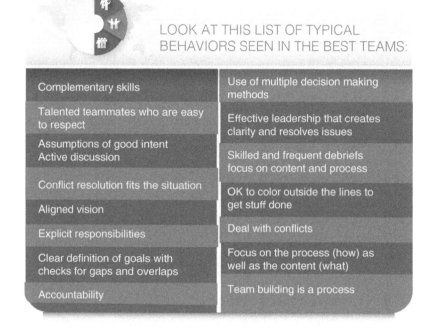

LOOK AT THIS LIST OF TYPICAL
BEHAVIORS SEEN IN THE BEST TEAMS:

Complementary skills	Use of multiple decision making methods
Talented teammates who are easy to respect	Effective leadership that creates clarity and resolves issues
Assumptions of good intent Active discussion	Skilled and frequent debriefs focus on content and process
Conflict resolution fits the situation	OK to color outside the lines to get stuff done
Aligned vision	
Explicit responsibilities	Deal with conflicts
Clear definition of goals with checks for gaps and overlaps	Focus on the process (how) as well as the content (what)
Accountability	Team building is a process

Figure 3.2 Best teams behaviors

In this case, it dawned on the CEO that, he, too, had dumbed down. He saw that if he and his leadership team weren't happy with the culture and the organization's performance, they had a responsibility to change it. They just needed the tools.

The behaviors that we accept and reward define an organization's culture. It is a powerful force. As Peter Drucker famously said, "Culture eats strategy for lunch."

So what kind of culture must we nurture if we're to see our strategies succeed? Here are the core elements I've observed across numerous companies over the years:

- mutual trust and respect;
- deep individual understanding and belief in the vision of the organization;

- a sense of shared purpose coupled with an alignment of action;
- intolerance at every level of office politics and the vigilance to see it;
- eagerness to solve hard problems by working in the white spaces as much as in our functional boxes.

The overwhelming reason Compaq doesn't exist as a corporation today is the change that occurred when the company's board suddenly ousted founder Rod Canion. The firm could not withstand the damage that the firing inflicted on the *foundation* of its culture.

Why? It wasn't just the loss of a beloved founder; other organizations have transitioned smoothly through that gate. It wasn't because the new strategy or culture was inherently different. Certainly, the new leadership didn't want the culture to dumb down.

In reality, the change caused decisions to be made very differently, from a distinct base, driven by a set of core values that allowed—and at times even encouraged—dumbing down and teamwork-as-usual. *Internal strategies stopped supporting external ones.*

Do you have a remedy to this potential draining dilemma? It's no off-the-shelf team-training workshop. It goes much deeper than that. Once you recognize the problem, here's what to do about it:

Create a Culture of No Dumbing Down

As a leader in your organization, you must:

- Value process as well as content.
  - It's not enough to get stuff done. *How* it gets done is as important. If you want an organization full of high-performing teamwork, value the disciplined process that supports it.
- Ask for what you want, notice what you get.
  - There's no substitute for describing your intentions to your organization. The more clarity, the more likely the 10,000 decisions that are made every day will be aligned with your vision.

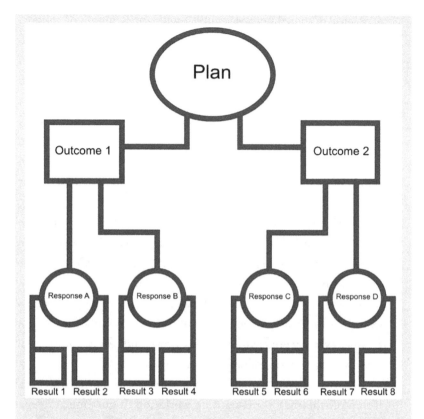

Once you describe your intentions, it's important you ensure you've communicated them effectively. All too often are directions misinterpreted because of ambiguous wording that the speaker assumes is obvious. Take this simple decision tree that most programmers use to diagram code. The initial input, or plan, is specifically defined. It clearly explains what are the necessary follow-ups based on the possible outcomes, and from there it begins to fracture into more and more possibilities, each clearly defined with its own explicit follow-up. See if you can use this same level of detail and clarity. Communication that goes this in-depth can make a huge difference in the quality of your staff's understanding.

- Notice! Be vigilant. Watch for dumbing down, the conditions that incubate it (politics, mismatched skills, etc.), and the signs that it's taking hold (straining vs. scaling, "active" disengagement, unplanned turnover, etc.).
- If you aren't getting what you want, hire and train the interpersonal skills necessary for successful teamwork. These include:
  - decision-making methods;
  - conflict-resolution skills;
  - debriefing as an integral part of everyday communications.

Reward the behaviors that you want.

- Rewards come in many flavors. Compensation certainly, but also increased recognition, trust, and responsibility.
- Reward behaviors, not technical skills alone. Make sure that your own consistently align with your intentions. Wanting things to be different isn't enough.
- Walk the talk. If there is variance in your own behavior, you can be sure that it will be reflected in the actions of your employees.

I recognize that it's hard to hire, lead, and manage thousands of employees with the same passion and alignment as you would in a start-up. But that doesn't mean you shouldn't try. It's demanding, not impossible.

And it must be done because dumbing down leads to exponential decreases in organizational productivity. With this in mind, what's an incremental increase in performance worth to your organization? Do you want to attract more A-players? Do you desire higher retention rates and less rework?

This is up to you, senior leader. Only you have the influence and authority to create the culture, the processes, and the discipline required to successfully prevent or root out the dumbing down of your organization.

Dumbing down is a cultural issue. If you don't dumb down, neither will your organization.

Make It Real

Now, jot down notes for yourself. Think about your organization. How are you promoting the best work? How are you creating high-performance opportunities for individuals and teams? How are you avoiding dumbing down in groups? Is there room for improvement? How will you hold yourself accountable?

_____

_____

_____

_____

_____

_____

_____

_____

_____

_____

_____

_____

_____

CHAPTER 4

Double Back

From Start-Up to Grown-Up (and Back Again)

I am not a product of my circumstances. I am a product of my decisions.
—Stephen Covey

The traditional model for business growth is *linear*. You may think of a few friends who have joined forces to found a start-up. They gain traction in the marketplace, begin growing in size, and eventually transition to a large-scale corporation. We've seen this happen countless times. It's the typical success story of many of today's top organizations—Microsoft, Apple, Facebook, Hewlett–Packard, even Disney.

That large-scale corporation becomes our goal, a measurement of success. The tight-knit group of visionaries has taken their brainchild and expanded it to national or international stature. Their products or services are being adopted on a mass scale; their sales force has ballooned, they may even be gaining influence within an industry. Who doesn't want to realize that kind of outcome?

As you might guess, the reality is never as clear-cut as we like to assume. There's a downside to this kind of growth.

Obstacles of all kinds can emerge in unforeseen ways. The culture evolves, procedures change, and departments expand. The strategies you used to build a business out of your garage don't serve you when you're trying to reach the next stage. As you grow, your organization will require new and improved tactics to continue thriving.

But the growth comes at what cost?

It's common to watch start-ups make it big, only to have the founder step down from his or her post. These leaders have often become disappointed or frustrated with their company's new direction. They remember the early days—days of just getting stuff done, of not taking "no" for an answer, of working overtime to pull off incredible feats. The scrappy, independent environment and culture they once knew have since transformed into a slow-moving administrative hell (Figure 4.1).

The model for success for evolving from a start-up to a mature company is necessary, but not sufficient. So what is the problem?

Just like people, businesses cycle through different stages of development. They begin as youthful, rambunctious ventures before they eventually transition into more mature organizations. The difference between you and your organization, though, is that you only grow in one direction.

We don't think this way about companies. We apply the same logic to our organizations that we do to ourselves. Our model for success assumes a linear and unidirectional trajectory—and is flat-out wrong.

We need a new model. We need one where an organization can accelerate its growth by shifting its developmental stage forward *and* backward.

An organization may not derive long-term, or even short-term, success by continuing to move toward what I like to call *grown-up mode*. This manner of operations is typically thought of as forward-leaning growth, most commonly seen in the later developmental stages of an organization.

Grown-up behavior in companies typically manifests itself as the standardization of processes, tools, and methods. In other words, your attitude as a business epitomizes standard operating procedure. Everything is by the book—for better or worse.

On the other side of the spectrum, we find the *start-up mode*. Here, you're operating by the seat of your pants. In exchange for little to no standardization, you have the space to be expedient and to innovate (Figure 4.2).

Each side of the continuum has its strengths. Start-up behavior requires highly responsive and collaborative teamwork. Once you're on the team, it's "welcome aboard" and "all hands on deck." Start-up ambitions are undefined and boundless. Compensation often includes rewards in the form of stock options. Getting results is a matter of survival, so start-up founders will fight tooth and nail to do whatever it takes to succeed.

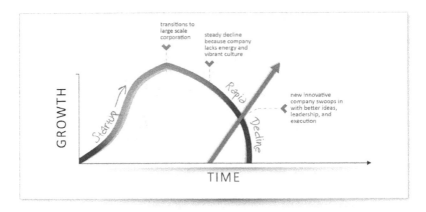

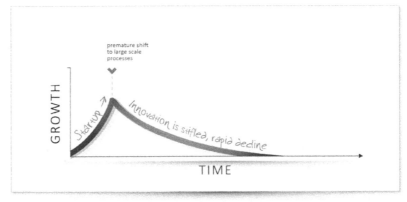

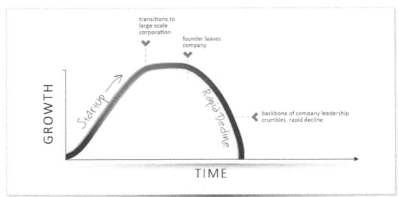

Figure 4.1 Growth and time

Figure 4.2 SOP continuum

The SOP Continuum can and should be applied to every function of an organization. However, because ventures like Compaq and IBM had such dramatically divergent methods of operation, it's easy to separate them as polar opposites. I entered Compaq when our staff numbered at only 104—every position was collaborative, fast paced, and hands-on. By contrast, IBM was grossing around $50 billion with almost half a million employees. They were highly bureaucratic with lagging processes. Our approaches to business were fundamentally different.

Compaq was envisioned as a big company in the formative stages. But alongside that, we wanted to be a good place to work—where our actions were aligned and understood by all. No more telling vendors you'd pay in net 30, only to have them begging for payment in 120 days. We knew which processes helped us grow, and which got in our own way.

On the contrary, grown-up behavior prizes regulation and careful planning. In exchange for a slower pace, managers have all their bases covered. If you work for an organization predominately functioning as a grown-up, chances are you applied in a large applicant pool, went through a lengthy interview process, and read through 50 pages of paperwork before any work could begin. Your organization has locations all over the country and occasionally risks minor litigation, so the paperwork was necessary. Thankfully, you and the rest of your team are legally protected. Not only that, but you know exactly when to expect your paycheck, and your health insurance is one of your benefits.

Similarly, start-up and grown-up operations each have downsides. If everyone you hire is a friend or neighbor, not only do you chance discrimination, but you can end up insulating your team from workers of diverse thought, background, and experience. The risks are also inherently higher in start-up mode. When you are doing something new, or in a new way, you have no precedent to follow.

A business operating in grown-up mode may find itself steeped in red tape. Red tape is always a way to stifle creativity, a quality that otherwise keeps any business afloat and relevant. In the grown-up mode, the risks are lower. This is great when you have slow, standardized processes for functions like ethical precautions or following regulations. But issues arise when you find yourself lacking expediency in a high-impact situation. In essence, grown-up organizations tend to work efficiently, but not necessarily *successfully*.

If you're wondering whether your organization or a division of your organization is functioning in grown-up mode, there's a great rule of thumb I like to use. Say your CEO's name is Jeff. If workers don't know why they're doing what they're doing because of a tangled mess of standardized processes, you'll hear the phrase "Jeff said," or "because Jeff told us too." Rather than grasping the rationale behind their contributions, workers will operate blindly in an organization with extreme grown-up behavior.

Notice, though, that there is zero correlation between these two types of behavior and the size of your organization, or its chronological age.

The difference between an organization in start-up or grown-up mode speaks entirely to the culture of your business and the mentality by which you operate. It's true that smaller operations can foster more seat-of-the-pants behavior, but that is not an exclusive privilege. Large-scale corporations can and do practice start-up behavior while maintaining their perspective.

Remember, because it's a continuum, that means this model is not a binary to toggle between, but a barometer to be adjusted. The processes, tools, and behaviors of every organization each fall in a different place on the continuum. Some are closer to start-up behavior; others are more grown-up oriented.

Consider these case studies.

COMPANY A

A few dozen colleagues are just months into the formation of their new insurance company. They've found some clients and are beginning to turn a profit. Up until now, workers have been informally compensated. One staff member has been writing individual checks as a way of distributing the business' income. This method, which embodies start-up culture, has been fast, easy, and inexpensive. But with a growing customer base, the company is looking to expand its workforce, a move that will further complicate this particular staff member's job. The company faces two options:

Option 1: They can continue the start-up behavior of writing and distributing checks manually. In the past, this tactic has been an easy and inexpensive incentive for employees to work hard and fast. But now, it may stifle efficiency to have one worker in charge of paycheck distribution for such a large group of employees—especially considering any necessary tax withholdings or deductions he or she will have to manage. In expanding their sales force, all manner of compensation and incentive structures must be considered.

OR

Option 2: They could shift to a centralized payroll system, which would mean hiring additional employees—or outsourcing—to form a payroll department. While this may be a costly move in the short term, it will allow the business to continue growing its workforce and long-term profits.

The company chooses option 2. It shifts its payroll processes from start-up to grown-up, capitalizing on the advantages of standardization. But notice that payroll is the *only* aspect of the company that makes this shift. In many cases, it's beneficial that the majority of a company's departments remain in start-up mode long after their internal operations become grown-up. A high-energy environment that encourages innovation was the primary catalyst to begin with—losing this kind of culture could jeopardize the growth in sales and your ability to fulfill those sales promises.

COMPANY B

An international tech organization is well established in its industry, but its sales have plateaued, and analysts predict the company will begin to decline if it does not make changes. Its board of directors has suggested that the firm scout for new business ventures to acquire, with the hope of feeding a start-up environment with enough resources to do extraordinary things. The senior leaders lock onto to a team of coders looking to launch a smartphone app that will reinvent personal finance. The coders meet with the management team and sign a contract.

Within a month, the organization has connected the coders with their firm's marketing department to design a social media campaign for the launch of their app. Initially, everything goes well—the coders seem wide-eyed and giddy after several brainstorming sessions. A week later, they all decide on a game plan, but the Director of Marketing explains that it's going to take 9 to12 months for the organization to begin implementing the campaign. The coders will have to wait for the tech organization's bureaucracy to do its job. With this news, the coders lose all excitement, and within a month, the coders walk out the door, and the venture collapses. Even those with work-out contract clauses are less than enthusiastic and not performing. They've dumbed down—just like we discussed in Chapter 3.

What began as an M&A turned into what I like to call an M&D, or "Merge and Destroy." What happened? A company still in the start-up stage was suffocated by an organization functioning predominately in grown-up mode. The team of coders was bogged down by the larger organization's lack of speed. Whatever free-spirited and innovative environment the senior leaders had previously created was now gone.

I'll often see an organization segregate their acquisitions, walling them off from the grown-up part of the organization. There is some value in this, but the synergies between teams and the infusion of new energy are lost. While it may be counterintuitive, the solution here would have been for the multinational tech organization to adopt a start-up approach in interacting with the team of coders. They could learn how to foster the team's enthusiasm by embodying this energy themselves. Maybe, they could have formed a group within their chain of command that specialized in pushing lengthy processes through faster.

COMPANY C

With some small investor funding, several graduate students decide to launch a new kind of sportswear that keeps you warm in winter. Right now, only a group of a few people runs sales, marketing, manufacturing, and customer relations. Their clientele ranges from local vendors to online shoppers.

The business has been using SurveyMonkey and Microsoft Excel to track the customer feedback. The information is entered manually by several different employees, who all help to analyze the data for trends and determine how to meet their customers' needs. The same team deals with customer support, answering the phones, and replying to emails. Given the firm's current size, this "seat-of-the-pants" approach is both feasible and cost effective.

At what point should their customer relations transform from start-up to a grown-up? When will their staff be spread too thin to manage all these responsibilities? When will they accumulate too much customer data to analyze? These are all signals that the team needs to reevaluate their approach and consider a more grown-up strategy.

As you might imagine, an organization that spends too much of its time and resources at any one point on the spectrum will begin to get stuck. It can manifest cross-organizationally or within just one department. Many of the businesses I work with find themselves in these circumstances.

For example, it's critical that COMPANY A keep an eye on the impacts its centralized payroll system will have on the size of its workforce.

The measures the firm has taken at this juncture may foster the right environment to grow the organization from a few dozens to a few thousand. But what happens when it reaches 3,000 employees? The tactics that moved the business out of its first stage of development might impede growth at the next level.

It's important for you to not only evaluate your business' processes, tools, and behaviors to see if they're getting in your way, but also to continue to *reevaluate* them at different stages of growth.

As we've seen, there are times in an organization's development where it makes the most sense for a firm to go backward, to shift procedure from grown-up to start-up. I call this strategy *doubling back.*

UPS embodied this perfectly during one of its busy holiday seasons. The team responsible for sorting, loading, and delivering packages was understaffed, leading to a last-minute scramble. Under a tight deadline to deliver packages in time for Christmas, the company pooled together workers from accounting, marketing, and other desk jobs to hit the streets. "Some [were] delivering packages using their personal vehicles," the *Wall Street Journal* reporter Paul Ziobro wrote.[1]

Who could imagine a $60 billion company pulling off this kind of team effort? It was a tremendous—albeit momentary—shift from grown-up to start-up. For about a week, the company collaborated with the same seat-of-the-pants drive I regularly observed at Compaq.

I remember when Compaq exceeded the $1 billion mark—our growing workforce was outpacing our office space and we had no intention of slowing down. Our solution was a great example of flexibility (a quintessential start-up competency). Without the time to wait for construction to finish on new buildings, we set up shop in one of our parking garages. We built a landing to level the angled flooring, set up walls, and assembled a walkway connected to the main building. Our goal was to continue expanding while not interrupting workflow. It worked.

These types of strategies emerge all the time in the heat of the moment. But more likely than not, when they do, we're not aware of what's happening. It should come as no surprise that identifying these

---

[1] P. Ziobro. December 26, 2017. "At UPS, It's All Hands On Deck," *The Wall Street Journal,* U.S. ed., Business section.

qualities of your organization is a great way to align internal and external strategies, and by so doing, to support your organization's growth.

How do you shift your organization from behaving unconsciously to consciously within this framework?

1. **Identify your coordinates.**

   Ask yourself, "Where are we?" Pinpoint all the functions of your business and examine from where on the SOP continuum they're operating. Now is a great time to sit down with the rest of the leadership team and practice clear communication to ensure everyone is on the same page (and avoid dumbed-down teamwork). You may be somewhere completely different from the other senior leaders, or you may all be operating with the same approach. Being explicit about these differences and similarities is a critical step to ensuring success. It will help you chart where you want to go and how to get there.

2. **Decide on a set of goals.**

   "Where do we want to be in 18 months? 2 years? 5 years?" If your aim is to double your organization's profits, figure out what processes will help you get there. Where might doubling back help your company? In what changes will you have the time, energy, and resources to invest? What changes may be too disruptive to your organization?

   Differentiating which start-up and grown-up functions need changing and which should remain as they are will depend on the kind of results you're seeking. If your goal is creativity and innovation, consider doubling back on your functions around product development and design. If you see your staff despondent and uninvested, consider taking another look at your workplace processes so your staff feels more influential and interconnected.

   Major shifts in your industry should also trigger the need for doubling back. In other words, use start-up behavior to capitalize on new opportunities in the market. Maybe your customers are asking for products or services you not only don't have, but don't know how to provide. Perhaps it's taking too long to deliver on some plans, either to appease customers or avoid rising competition. These are all situations where doubling back on aspects of your business may open up a treasure trove of new directions forward.

3. **Examine doubling back functionally and cross-functionally.**

    "What will be the ramification of these changes? Where are our resources being relocated, and what effects will that have on each department and the organization as a whole?" Consider how your team will prioritize doubling back strategies over others. Where would you like to create synergy? What's that going to take? Who needs to be involved, who needs to be informed? Who will this impact?

4. **Make a game plan.**

    Each senior leader will need different things from the rest of the team to ensure his or her success. For instance, the processes, tools, and behaviors of accounting will need to function differently than that of sales. It will be critical that each senior leader understands where on the SOP continuum his division will need to be, or what kind of processes, tools, and behaviors he will need to adopt. One division may be operating primarily as a start-up, while another may be in grown-up mode. Communication here will be critical.

5. **Execute the plan and track your progress.**

    As I mentioned earlier, it's critical that you continually measure your success. Many of the businesses I work with begin executing these internal strategies, but either something gets poorly implemented or there's an external shift, which makes for some unexpected outcomes. While your aim should be to avoid these situations, you need to be prepared. Nothing ever goes exactly according to plan. Tracking your organization's success will allow you to respond to unforeseen circumstances with greater ease and learn from your mistakes. You should always try to understand what got you where you are. Your team will need to track your organization in real time.

    Decide what metrics you should be reviewing: what data are most important to your success and the success of your team? What kind of short-term and long-term success are you seeking and how is measuring each different? Use your organization's dashboard to automate as much of this as you can. It's a great idea to convene a quarterly retreat for senior leaders to examine and reevaluate intentions and outcomes.

This kind of strategy is a grown-up behavior in itself—it requires patience, care, and lots of coordination. But if your organization can begin operating with this deeper awareness, accelerated growth will not only become possible, but probable, too. You'll be able to define your goals, minimize your weaknesses, and have a clearer view of your trajectory.

Add to this the ability to be agile and suddenly your organization is a force with which to be reckoned.

But wait—that's just one word. What does it mean to be *agile*?

The story began in 2001 when a group of software development experts gathered at a ski resort in Utah to discuss innovative business practices. They left with a manifesto—the Agile Manifesto (Figure 4.3). It was a structure of values that would go on to redefine the priorities of many tech companies, as well as many other growing industries. Here it is.

It's a simple document, but one with radical implications. Even if you aren't a software developer, there's value to be mined. I'd like to highlight the last point: *responding to change* over *following a plan* is how I define agility. Expect the unexpected. Adapt.

This kind of agility is critical for doubling back. I guarantee your plans won't always work out as expected, especially when you're growing

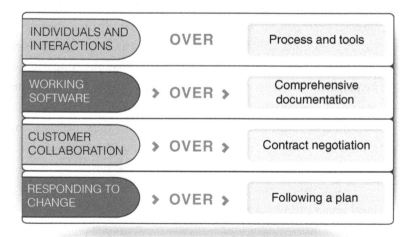

Figure 4.3 The agile manifesto

Source: Kent Beck, Mike Beedle, Arie van Bennekum, Alistair Cockburn, Ward Cunningham, Martin Fowler, James Grenning, Jim Highsmith, Andrew Hunt, Ron Jeffries, Jon Kern, Brian Marick, Robert C. Martin, Steve Mellor, Ken Schwaber, Jeff Sutherland, and Dave Thomas, "Manifesto for Agile Software Development," 2001.

or shifting the culture of your organization. Dealing with unanticipated consequences is an invaluable skill set. But what's required?

The answer isn't simple. Staying agile is a methodology in its own category. It demands its unique framework, internal processes, and measurements for success. And yet it is a core element of any thriving organization, as well as one of my five internal strategies.

Keep reading to learn how and why an agile organization is a healthy organization.

Make It Real

Time for more notes! Consider the operations that you oversee. Where on the SOP continuum would you place your staff's behavior? How are you optimizing or weighing down the organization by your processes? Is there any helpful information you could get from the other senior leaders? What kind of communication is necessary between you, your peers, and the staff you manage?

_____

_____

_____

_____

_____

_____

_____

_____

_____

_____

_____

_____

_____

CHAPTER 5

Play Bumper Cars

Why Agility Matters and How to Achieve It

Never be so faithful to your plan that you are unwilling to consider the unexpected. Never be so faithful to your plan that you are unwilling to entertain the improbable opportunity that comes looking for you.
—Elizabeth Warren

Let's backtrack for a second. What *exactly* does growth look like for an organization? What happens when you find a strategy that works?

A lot can happen. Different facets of your organization can expand, shrink, demand attention, or lose value. Your customer base can shift from one demographic to another. Your business model may need revising. Maybe your competitors steal your ideas. Will you anticipate all of this before it happens? No, of course not. The common denominator across all growing organizations is the unexpected.

What if you're not growing? It's the same story! In fact, if your organization's growth has plateaued, you're even more susceptible to the effects of unexpected change. Outside innovation becomes an even more dangerous threat. The risk of becoming less relevant looms larger and larger as more groundbreaking ideas and practices surface in your market. (A stagnant business is a business in decline. If you remain where you are, you're sliding backward within your market. Just something to consider!)

So how do you plan for the unplanned? The answer is you can't, at least not in the way you would think. You need a different skill set. You need to be *agile*.

I define agility based on The Agile Manifesto, which I introduced in the last chapter. If your organization is agile, you have the flexibility to react to unanticipated circumstances, whether challenges or opportunities.

A great analogy here is bumper cars. Imagine your organization is seated in one car, seat belt buckled, and helmeted. You whiz around the arena bumping into walls and other cars. The question is are you bouncing in every which way, haphazardly arriving wherever physics takes you, or do you premeditate your trajectory and use the laws of motion to determine your course?

If you find your organization ricocheting or always rushing to react to circumstances as they arise, you may benefit from a more formal approach.

I bring up physics for a reason here. The reality is that the motion of bumper cars can be analyzed as a science—the mass of the automobiles, their momentum, the arena's friction, each car's velocity, the list goes on. If you can identify every variable in the equation, you suddenly can take a guess at what might happen if you hit objects in your path. This is the essence of an agile organization. Not only will you have foresight, but you will react quickly to unforeseen outcomes. Challenges will pose less of a threat, and your ability to take advantage of opportunities will increase.

Take the example of Blockbuster. What an unnecessary catastrophe.

In its prime, the video rental provider had worldwide operations: it spread everywhere from the United States to Israel to Brazil. By 2000, the company was taking in almost $800 million in late fees *alone*. And then one particular customer—who happened to be a Silicon Valley software engineer and entrepreneur—got particularly frustrated when an overdue rental of *Apollo 13* landed him a $40 fine.[1]

The model changed, along with customer expectations. Why drive down to the local Blockbuster to thumb through a shelf of DVDs in person when you could hop on the computer and have them delivered to your house? Netflix, Redbox, and other on-demand video services had sprung to the top of the market. Despite their attempts to catch up, Blockbuster filed for bankruptcy by 2010.[2]

---

[1]Netflix.

[2]M. Phillips and R. A. Ferdman. November 6, 2013. "A Brief, Illustrated History of Blockbuster, Which is Closing the Last of Its US Stores," *Quartz.*

Blockbuster illustrates how an organization that's unresponsive to changing circumstances can crumble. The company had grown massively since its founding in 1985, but its demise pointed to a tremendous frailty within the organization. Over several years, a competitor emerged selling the same product with a sleeker business model. The innovation was a step in the right direction, and yet Blockbuster paid too little attention, too late. The video rental company could have had a happy ending. With an agile infrastructure capable of effectively responding, it could have easily participated in the market's shift to on-demand models.

There's no doubt Blockbuster had the resources for it. The business' issue wasn't feasibility; it was agility. The company lacked the flexibility and leadership to follow the shift.

It's also worthwhile to note that Blockbuster demonstrated poor resiliency (a competency all agile organizations wield with strength). As Netflix and Redbox zoomed to the top of the market, Blockbuster realized it was behind the curve, still employing yesterday's business model. But its attempt to adopt the DVD-by-mail and rental kiosk services posed little threat. The company's shift over to the new model was tremendously overdue and lacked vision. Blockbuster's attempt at a comeback mustered nowhere near the momentum it needed to get back on its feet.[3]

Now consider the polar opposite. *The New York Times* stands out as a shining example of agility. The newspaper is over 150 years old, yet it is not only afloat, but still a prestigious name in its industry. When the Internet hit, everyone was predicting the newspaper business would die. There was and still is never-ending talk of how digitalization and public access to information pose a continual threat to print publications. But as early as 1996, the *Times* began adopting digital publication methods, and by 2005 offering online subscriptions. Seven years later, you were able to get *The New York Times* on your iPhone or iPad.[4]

The difference here between Blockbuster and the *Times* is glaring. An organization reliant on print publications noticed a radical shift to online

---

[3]G. Satell. September 21, 2014. "A Look Back At Why Blockbuster Really Failed And Why It Didn't Have To," *Forbes Magazine.*
[4]"Our History," *The New York Times Company,* 2018.

media. The *Times* saw a world where information was flooding in on laptops and smartphones, rather than on paper. Its bumper car had hit a major obstacle and was flying in a dramatically different direction that anyone could have predicted. The Internet was becoming more and more ubiquitous, trashing business models right and left. The *Times's* response was to embrace—and lead—the change.

While its agility required lots of reconfiguration, it also benefited from explicit goal setting. An organization like *The New York Times* would not have been able to succeed by simply encouraging its infrastructure to adopt new intentions. Being agile demands concrete strategy.

It also demands flexibility and a tolerance for ambiguity. You'll remember from the last chapter that both of these are important competencies of start-up behavior. That isn't a coincidence. Many pathways to growth come from organizations doubling back by innovating one or many aspects of their business. An agile organization that's turning an unexpected outcome into an opportunity will often benefit from going backward. The reason many organizations struggle to do this is due to the strategy's lack of control. Remember, grown-up mode is standardized. Every function of a mature organization has processes of all kinds to make sure everyone knows exactly what they're doing and how to do it. Processes provide a lot of certainty—as a senior leader, you know what's expected of you and your workers.

But if you double back to start-up mode, suddenly things become pretty uncertain. You're operating in a space without many processes or rules. Your options expand exponentially, and your behavior is entirely up to you. Frankly, that can be scary for some people.

The flip side here is the freedom to push boundaries, take risks, and innovate. But how do you mitigate the uncertainty? How do you avoid floating in space, hoping and praying you aren't inadvertently jeopardizing your organization?

It's time to return to bumper cars. The answer is *guardrails*. An organization must be open to ambiguity to be at all agile. But you can ensure you feel safe taking risks by setting up boundaries for yourself. Guardrails create a contained space within which your organization can bounce back and forth. Here's the step-by-step methodology I've developed.

1. **Where do you place the guardrails?**

   You first need to define your goals. "Where am I and where do I want to go?" Obviously, your aim should be up and to the right in one way or another. You want to invest resources in strategies that offer high impact with a high likelihood of success (more on this later!) (Figure 5.1).

   Next, use your guardrails to create a space in which to play. Establish the limits of your organization's capabilities. Where are the constraints in your budget? What's your cash flow? How about your turnover rate? Take a look at your overall business metrics to see what kind of flexibility you have. Create an upper guardrail for the fastest growth your organization could theoretically sustain. Then, do the same for the lower guardrail—what's the least amount of growth your organization needs to ensure it stays healthy?

   And remember, the environment within your organization can also have significant impacts. When deciding on where to place your guardrails, make sure you account for outside influences—the kind that organizations like Blockbuster failed to address.

2. **Measure your strategy's success and watch reality take hold.**

   Then you run with it. Begin implementing whatever strategies you've determined will push you toward your goals. Maybe your new one is rocket fuel, and your organization's growth starts climbing much faster than you first estimated. It's so fast you that hit your upper guardrail. One option here is to pull back because you don't have the resources to sustain the growth (Figure 5.2).

Figure 5.1 Guardrails

Figure 5.2 Hitting the Top Guardrail

From here, you'll most likely watch your trajectory bounce off the upper guardrail and begin heading toward the lower guardrail. I call this process *upside flexibility.* It's all very normal. At this point, the opposite will happen. You'll begin approaching the other extreme, whereby you've slowed down your growth enough to avoid overextending what resources you have, while also keeping your organization healthy and high performing. Once you hit that lower guardrail, you'll want to bounce off to avoid continuing in that direction as well. In other words, to evade underperforming as a business, you'll want to engage whatever strategy will direct your trajectory back up in the direction of the upper guardrail. I refer to this as *downside flexibility* (Figure 5.3).

I'll tell you right now that no organization will exactly follow that middle line. Expect to stray from your estimates. In fact, it's likely your metrics will begin bouncing between the upper and lower guardrails. Be prepared to exercise both upside and downside flexibility, increasing or decreasing growth to match what your organization is capable of sustaining.

Flexibility should be ringing a few bells. In essence, these guardrails represent the threshold at which point your internal and external strategies become misaligned. Hitting the upper guardrail means the results you're getting are outpacing your ability to perform—imagine a business who's sold more products than their capable of delivering on time. On the opposite side of the spectrum, hitting the lower guardrail means you are overperforming internally and are unable to garner the desired results that could happen to a business, which has manufactured more products than its workforce is capable of selling.

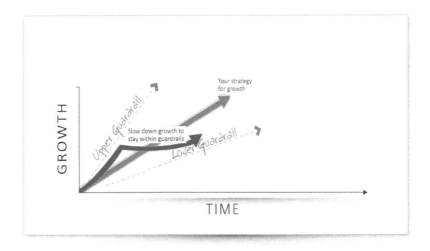

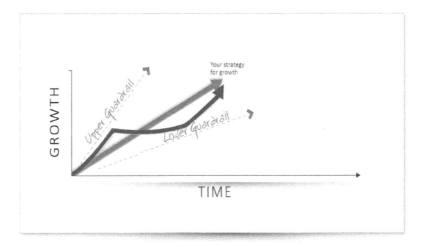

Figure 5.3 Using the Guardrails

Hopefully, you're catching on to why I love this bumper car analogy so much. And you can understand why visualizing your growth can be tremendously helpful.

Staying agile like this requires you and your senior leadership team to exhibit an overarching awareness. It means continually measuring the success of your strategy and adjusting where you allocate your resources based on where you end up at each stage of the process.

3. **Redraw your roadmap.**

   But say you're hitting the upper guardrail, and you have the extra resources to accommodate the new growth. You may have the money to hire new staff, expand to a new location, release more products, or begin contracting with larger clients. Now you have the opportunity to reset your guardrails.

   But let me remind you to account for external factors. Innovations of all kinds can completely skew your progress and catapult you to somewhere you would have never expected. While measuring internal metrics is a must, devote substantial time to monitoring where the rest of the market is. How are your competitors behaving? What's the media saying? Have there been any new developments in technology, politics, or the economy that might affect your business? Something outside your organization like this may warrant redrawing your guardrails, either to prepare for complications or to capitalize on favorable circumstances (Figure 5.4).

   Ideally, you'd like your organization to continually rise to new levels of growth, which would mean revising your guardrails to align with larger and larger amounts of expansion. You can imagine why measuring your success and reevaluating your strategy are critical to any of this working.

You are now beginning to understand how an agile organization can determine its growth, while also accounting for unexpected outcomes.

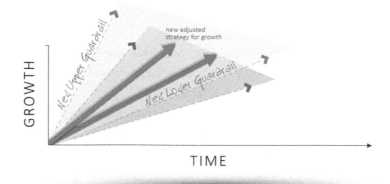

Figure 5.4 *Guardrails with new upper and lower rails*

Let's circle back to deciding which strategies are worth your investment. You won't get far without this piece of the puzzle.

To choose the best strategy, you want to zoom out and consider all possible scenarios. Sounds daunting, right? There's a quick shortcut for this.

The value of all potential strategies that may grow your business can be boiled down to two variables: *impact* and *likelihood*. I mentioned earlier that you'll always want to funnel resources into plans that are likely to work and offer high impact. Pretty simple stuff, I know. But visualizing all of this in a handy-dandy 2 × 2 matrix can help differentiate between resources well spent and wasted investments (Figure 5.5).

Picture a car manufacturer that's tracking the rise of electric motors. Over the last few months, they've observed Tesla cars gaining more and more popularity. After conducting some large-scale surveys, they've found that the primary complaint of Tesla owners is the cost of their vehicle. With this information in mind, the car manufacturer begins designing an electric car with all the same capabilities but at a substantially lower cost than any Tesla model.

Reducing costs is a useful example of a high impact and high likelihood strategy. The company has already found an emergent market for electric cars, so the likelihood of them gaining traction is high—especially given that Tesla already has very few competitors who offer the same intelligent design. If it is successful, it could cause a massive boost in sales and become Tesla's most successful product launch. In other words, high impact.

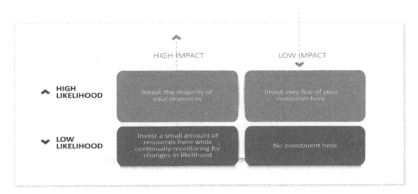

Figure 5.5 High- and low-impact matrix

However, low-impact and high likelihood strategies should not consume much of your time, money, and labor. While small victories may be beneficial, you'll want to direct most of your attention elsewhere.

Similarly, high-impact and low likelihood strategies should only eat up a small number of your resources. However, this is another great place to continually measure and monitor, just as you would evaluate the strategy in which you're investing the most. Say there's a new technology being developed that, when combined with your business model, could potentially double your sales. The issue is, there's very little information on when this technology is going to be available for commercial use, and rumors suggest it may never happen. It's still a solid idea to place a small number of resources here. In the off chance that it will release commercially in the future, you'll want to be able to capitalize on its high impact.

Working at Compaq taught me much of what I've just described, but there was one particular philosophy I've found to be critical. Amidst all the chaos of working under tight deadlines and making sure we had the resources to support our rapid expansion, we always were able to continue our high performance in ambiguous circumstances. I think this offers unique insight into the power of being an agile organization.

It was Compaq's leadership that created this kind of culture. All the leading executives understood that to survive and flourish, we would have to travel into uncharted waters. Venturing into the unknown meant, at its core, tolerating ambiguity. It was half skill, half character—we had to embody this competency to lead with it.

What I mean here is that there's only one way for you to lead your organization into ambiguous territory. And that's to be comfortable in that space yourself. If you can't function in that kind of environment, your organization won't be able to either.

Remember one of the basic tenets of leadership—you can only lead from where you are. If you personify where you want your organization to be, your staff can follow along.

Make It Real

Are you ready for more notes? Start by listing the primary goals of your organization. What would you like to achieve by next quarter or next year? What kind of resources would it take to get there? What kind of collaboration from your fellow senior leaders would this require? How could you and your team prepare one another and the rest of your organization for doubling back? What kind of leadership tactics would you use to ensure your staff continued to perform well in ambiguous circumstances?

_____

_____

_____

_____

_____

_____

_____

_____

_____

CHAPTER 6

Become a Utility

Make the Sale, Now Flip the Switch

Each problem that I solved became a rule, which served afterwards to solve other problems.

—René Descartes

While the Agile Manifesto points to the power of responsive and customer-focused work, there's an underlying implication that should not go ignored.

Take a look at the phrasing. The creators could have written, "individuals and interactions, *not* process and tools." Instead, they phrased it as "individuals and interactions *over* process and tools." The insinuation here is rather significant. While individuals and interactions may be superior to process and tools, these two items should not be discounted. Processes play an essential role in a thriving organization. They build a foundation from which to grow.

Let's examine this in context. In the last chapter, we covered agility—how best to harness the unexpected to grow your business. But isn't growth inherently disruptive? How does an organization maintain a stable foundation as its resources expand and its needs change?

The answer, as you might've guessed, lies in processes. Standardizing operations will help you create your organization's bedrock. It will do away with the fires you find yourself fighting again and again, and allow you and your senior team the freedom to direct your gaze toward the future. The MIT professor and author, Peter Senge, put it rather well, "If you reward fire-fighting, you get a lot of fires."[1]

---

[1] P.M. Senge. 2006. *The Fifth Discipline: The Art & Practice of The Learning Organization,* Revised & updated ed. (New York: Doubleday).

Some organizations devote a task force to this. Usually titled the Organizational Effectiveness Function, the group's goal is to eliminate any inefficiencies or recurring problems. They comb through the different processes of their organization and mine the data to determine what can be further optimized. This kind of team is great, but I recommend you take things a step further. What I look for in a healthy organization are processes that operate with routine efficiency.

I call this strategy functioning as a *utility*. I often give my clients the metaphor of a light switch—you roll out of bed in the morning and, without thinking, flip the switch. You don't waste any brain power on lighting the room. A light switch has one job, and it does it well; this is the nature of a utility.

To establish the bedrock of your business, there will need to be processes within your organization that work the same way. There's no doubt you'll need to fight many fires as you grow. Some of them will be unavoidable.

If you can begin creating processes within your organization that function as a utility, you will be able to mitigate many of these disruptive issues.

For a process within your organization to function as a utility, it must embody specific criteria. Let's explore the "what" and "why" of each.

The Four Traits of a Utility

1. **Efficiency**

   Efficiency should be pretty straightforward. The reason for converting any process into a utility is to create consistent reliability, so that everyone involved can shift their focus elsewhere and to more important concerns. It should be efficient enough that it allows you that freedom. The simple on–off methodology of a light switch is a quintessential example.

2. **Flexibility**

   Because the definition of growth is positive change, you'll need to design your processes so they're able to accommodate these changes. I recommend you periodically review your methods to ensure they're still delivering the results you want. Things may need tweaking as your organization evolves. For example, it's easy to flip a switch, but how is the energy powered? Is it coal? Gas? Nuclear? Solar? Initially, coal could be your best option because of cost, but as you grow, you may realize that solar benefits your eco-friendly brand and strengthens customer loyalty.

3. **Replicability**

   For a process to function as a utility, it must be repeatable. If you're fidgeting with how you do things every time, it undermines any efficiency—and can often lead to confused or upset customers. This is the power of standardization. A utility will operate the same way every time, which will please you and your workers. It will also satisfy your customers if they're a part of the process. Uniformity allows for trust and reliability while doing away with unnecessary problem solving. Think about every hotel room you've ever been in—no matter what it looks like, the light switch is always at the same height on a wall, performing the same function.

4. **Scalability**

   It should come as no surprise that the purpose of creating utilities within your organization is to mitigate many of the issues that arise with expanding your operations. As a result, a utility must be able to grow alongside your business. No matter what you're lighting—be it a bathroom or a stadium—the electronics are always triggered by a switch. Even in the case of voice recognition technology like Amazon's Alexa do we arrive at the same utility model. Using Alexa is equivalent to outsourcing the process of turning on the light switch to a third party, a system that allows for the same routine functionality and scalability of a utility. (You'll hear more on outsourcing in a moment!)

If you're thinking how similar this all sounds to grown-up behavior, don't worry, you're on the right track. Just like there's a spectrum between *start-up* and *grown-up* (as we saw in the SOP continuum), there's also a spectrum between *agility* and *utility*. In fact, you could even say they're the same. Functions of an organization must be agile to innovate and grow, but other departments must act as a utility to support this growth with consistency and stability. This balance allows your organization to root itself in the ground ,while also reaching toward new heights of innovation.

Maintaining balance depends on why not every process within your organization should function as a utility. There are several ways to gauge what strategies warrant this optimization.

Consider creating a threshold for problems that arise within your organization. Convene a meeting with your senior leaders and discuss what fires you and others are always fighting. Some issues may not be worth your time to address. Others may be more impactful. For difficulties that fall into this category, graph out their frequency. If the number of times a difficulty arises crosses a certain threshold, you should consider turning it into a utility (Figure 6.1).

Different problems will require different thresholds, which will depend on the degree to which each issue is compromising your success and taking your focus away from what's important. For example, there may be a challenge you deal with on a regular basis, but its impact is so low, and it takes so little time to solve that it doesn't threaten your performance. In other situations, it may make sense to outsource specific functions of your organization. You may consider this if your organization is on the smaller size. It's a quick, hands-off solution, and a great idea if you're expanding rapidly and don't want to have to deal with strategizing for expansion.

In essence, outsourcing is a way to pay for flexibility and scalability. As we grew, Compaq had thousands of temporary employees. Rather than managing all that ourselves, we outsourced the process to various hiring agencies. The agencies functioned as utilities themselves. It became a central aspect of how we ran our business.

FREQUENCY
OF PROBLEM

threshold for
creating a utility

TIME

Figure 6.1 Thresholds

The flip side to this tactic, however, was the control we handed over to the agencies with which we contracted. Because outsourcing instantly converts that particular function into a utility, it loses its agility in exchange. The same is true for any process you transform into a utility. This is why it's important that certain functions do *not* become one—as we covered in the last chapter, there are substantial reasons why particular aspects of your organization must remain agile.

Making a process function as a utility can sometimes be as easy as a simple discovery. Have you ever realized that a job that took several people to complete could be executed by just one person? Other times, though, it will require more thought.

A core competency of a utility lies in the staff that helps execute its function. You want employees who get satisfaction out of doing things efficiently rather than employees who enjoy working creatively, which should be a large factor to consider when choosing who will help with these processes. You don't want an innovative manager redesigning your shipping procedure in the middle of a delivery.

But why list everything out when I can give an example with which we're all familiar?

Henry Ford's automobile assembly line is the epitome of a utility. In 1913, Ford took a process that was taking 12 hours and scaled it down to just two and a half. Initially using a rope-and-pulley powered conveyor belt, Ford's workers were able to manufacture the famous Model T car in a continuous flow. A few months later and they updated to a mechanized conveyor belt capable of covering as much as 6 feet/ minute. As they amassed millions of customers, the same assembly line production methods proved successful not only because of efficiency but because of scalability, as well.

And yet, what's worth noting is that Ford failed to synthesize the all-important balance of agility and utility. In the mid-1920s, about 10 years after his large-scale success, he began to see a decline in customers. Too intensely focused on elongating the popularity of the Model T, the entrepreneur missed where the market was heading. Consumers wanted inexpensive automobiles that featured more features than what Ford was offering.[2] But alas, the historical tycoon missed the boat—or car.

---

[2]History.com Staff. 2009. "Ford's assembly line starts rolling," *History.com.*

Here's another instance that's a bit more modern.

For most businesses, onboarding is one of the most expensive and demanding processes with which they deal. In some cases, the sales force will develop its strategy for what works. The issue is that the sales people sometimes don't communicate this to the rest of the organization. Suddenly, the sales force is describing products, explaining services, or making promises that the other departments can't possibly fulfill. Maybe sales people guarantee two-day shipping when in reality it takes 10 days. Now the organization suddenly risks disappointing customers and degrading loyalty.

This disconnect in customer expectations is common across numerous industries, and it poses a legitimate threat to customer bases everywhere. You can transform the processes of sales, manufacturing, and delivery into utilities without compromising their flexibility—because, after all, each of your clients will have slightly different needs that you'll want to accommodate.

All of this comes back to aligning internal and external strategies. Standardizing these processes will ensure that the sale is representative of what your business can offer customers.

You may find your business has already turned various departments into utilities. It's common for an executive to create an efficient and routine procedure for something he has had a bad experience with in the past. That bad experience has become a hot button for him, so he develops a high level of efficiency around it to ensure it never happens again. It could be anything from requiring new employees to undergoing an orientation or creating a template for client contracts. While it's always great to learn from our mistakes, this phenomenon is usually more subconscious than anything else. Intentionally and explicitly converting processes into utilities is where real optimization happens.

I worked with a market research firm several years ago by the name of Schlesinger Associates. They were a family business who had built themselves from the ground up and were highly successful masters at getting clients in the door. But as they grew, they realized they didn't have the internal infrastructure to support their success. To create the proper standardized backend processes, the CEO brought in an executive with a background in finance and hospitality as President. They formed a true partnership and with their complementary skills, they led the company to exponential growth.

Of course, no strategy frees your organization from any and all turbulence. Fires will break out regardless of where you are or what you're doing. You can use utilities to address these fires proactively or reactively. You can also send in firefighters. Often, you'll have to rely on all three tactics.

It's all part of surviving and thriving, and it follows the same tenets of the evaluating and reevaluating that I covered in the earlier chapters. Standardize your foundational processes, evaluate your successes, learn from your mistakes, and change accordingly.

Make It Real

It's time for note taking again. Imagine what fires come up for you and your organization all the time. Which ones are the most obnoxious? Inconvenient? Tedious? Which ones have the largest impact on productivity? Now take a look at where this problem originates. What would it take to create an optimized process to straighten out the issue? How could you work with your fellow senior leaders to address this fire and others? Are there any processes in your organization right now that could easily be turned into a utility without expending many resources?

_____

_____

_____

_____

_____

_____

_____

_____

CHAPTER 7

Learn to Levitate

Operate in the Meta Zone

How am I going to live today in order to create the tomorrow I'm committed to?

—Tony Robbins

I've now covered four strategies that are all indispensable to any organization looking to stay healthy and grow. They present tools for managing, mitigating, and manipulating every scenario for success—both the fine-tuning and the massive overhauls. So what's missing?

The implementation.

We've discussed all the theory you'll ever need, but at what point do you sit down and start making decisions? My fifth and final strategy lays out the framework for doing just that. It's simple, digestible, and doesn't require many resources other than time and energy. The catch? It's personal.

Working smarter and not harder means juggling lots of variables. Concrete and actionable planning is necessary for success—but it's not sufficient. True success eventually boils down to the person whom you present. Ask yourself, "How do I make decisions? How do I manage my time? How do I invest in the long term?" Your responses to each of these will radically impact your success.

I'm referring to the big picture. It's a daunting conversation for anyone to have, especially senior leaders. (If you or your team struggle with this, chances are good there's room for improvement.) I call this final strategy *levitating*, which is the ability to escape daily mundane activity and examine *everything* that's going on around you. To levitate, you must be able to step away from your limiting beliefs to look at the past, present, and future. You must be able to operate in the *meta zone*. In other words, you must be able to examine your organization from a vantage point that can perceive blind spots, hidden opportunities, unexpected challenges, and other impactful factors. Levitating is one of the most proactive and rewarding steps to success an individual or an organization can take.

I'm sure you're thinking, "We already do this on our annual retreats!" But I'm here to tell you that retreats are not enough, not in this day and age. The speed at which industries are evolving and innovating is itself speeding up. Take a look at Moore's Law, which has been successfully predicting that computing power is exponentially increasing as the necessary size of the hardware that houses the technology is exponentially decreasing.[1] The simple truth is that our world is changing too rapidly for an annual summit to be effective (Figure 7.1).

The obvious solution to this is to increase the frequency of your higher-level discussions. However, levitating goes deeper than this. It knocks you out of your daily fog and takes you to a higher level of awareness and intention. Let me explain what I mean.

We've talked about how to address disruption in the last four chapters—each strategy uniquely covered how to make sure your internal processes are aligned with external circumstances (what's going on outside your organization that may alter your trajectory?). But how do you superimpose these strategies onto your day-to-day operations? When and where does the decision making happen?

Many of my clients find themselves bogged down by the particulars of a current hurdle, which is our default reaction. We develop laser-focus for tackling a devised plan. It comes from our problem-solving nature that's been pounded into our heads and reinforced since Day One. Succeeding in any position demands these kinds of skills. If this is something at which you excel, that's fantastic. But we need to recognize the downside.

As we cultivate our expertise as problem solvers, we begin to *only* operate in this mindset. We start to rely too heavily on this strength and lose sight of the wider perspective. When massive disruption affects our organization, we're suddenly disoriented and unprepared. Or, worse, we

---

[1] "Moore's Law." *Investopedia*, November 24, 2003.

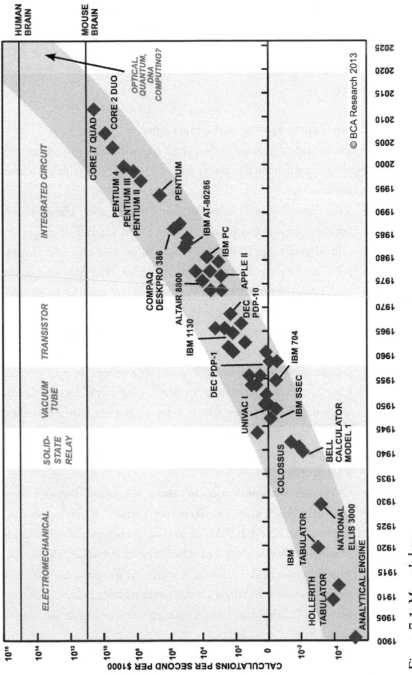

Figure 7.1 Moore's law

react to the crisis with strategies that worked for an isolated situation, but have no proven application outside that context.

To avoid this hyperfocus, you need to make time to step away from just checking off boxes and take a macroscopic view of what's going on. Here's how:

1. **Create time to operate in the meta zone.**

   As the driver of change within your organization, you, of course, need to stay responsive to unexpected circumstances, which is a great promise to make, but how do you do it?

   - Take control of your calendar. Every organization out there will ask more of you and your time than you're capable of giving. It's critical you make time. Not only will no one schedule this for you, but others will ask to impose on this time. Stay strong and understand the necessary investment you're making in yourself and your organization.

   - Devoting time to operate in the meta zone can look different for everyone—there is no one-size-fits-all prescription. Some people need an hour once a week. For others, it may take an hour *just to clear their heads*, in which case they'll need to devote a full day. Some prefer sitting alone at home or in their office. Others love having company off whom to bounce their ideas. These are all different parameters to experiment with and see what works.

   - Of course, sometimes you can't make it happen. There's a company emergency, some unforeseen work arises, or maybe someone needs you at home. It's ok! Scheduling these sessions will provide much more value than not scheduling them at all. Remember what Thoreau said, "Routine is a ground to stand on, a wall to retreat to; we cannot draw on our boots without bracing ourselves against it."[2] Levitating should become a frequent practice, not an isolated event.

---

[2]O. Shephard, ed. 1961. *The Heart of Thoreau's Journals,* 1st ed. (New York: Dover Publications, 1961).

- Practicing levitating holds true both for you and your senior team. I recommend finding time once a quarter where you and your team have the ability to sit down and discuss big picture topics. It can be as simple as one day offsite where everyone's laptops are closed, and phones are off. Getting into a rhythm with these kinds of meetings will create a new level of clarity—you should be able to identify ways to align your internal strategies, collaborate on problem-solving, and reflect on new directions for your organization.

2. **Ask questions.**

   Consistently mapping out all the different facets of your organization, your agreed-upon plans, and expectations of some disruptions will ensure that you run into as few surprises as possible. As I've said before—you can't plan for everything. But it's always better to ask more questions, rather than fewer.

   - Taking the time to think is so important. There are so many variables to consider when growing a business; in addition, you have to contend with the unexpected. None of it can be dealt with passively. To levitate, you must be able to actively understand your environment and how you're operating within it.

3. **Say no to shiny, new objects.**

   Make sure you don't fall into the abundance trap. We face so many choices in every waking moment of our day that we sometimes end up spending a significant amount of time making insignificant decisions. Many of us end up adding activities into our lives that are shiny and enjoyable, but hardly rewarding.

   - If you remember that your time is finite, you'll also recall that your goal is to get as big a bang for your buck as possible. So, it should make sense that mindlessly accumulating vain abundance can grow to be a burden on your productivity. I'm sure you've heard this before.
   - Avoiding the abundance trap is a direct byproduct of stepping back to reprioritize or levitating. When you operate in the meta zone, you're able to recognize what your primary goals and obligations are. You have the opportunity to reconfigure your commitments and how you spend your time. This is a helpful way to explicitly define what your internal strategies are (what

you and your organization is spending time on) and how well they're aligned with your external processes (the kind of results you're getting from your market).

4. **Develop your staff.**

While levitating is very much a personal strategy, it's weakened by self-reliance. As a senior leader, you should be high performing *and* collaborative. All too often I'll hear from my clients, "I can't take time off because no one else can do the work I need to get done." Or sometimes, "I could give this to my staff, but they have enough to do already." It's a common thought process, but it eliminates opportunities for both you and your staff.

- It may be counterintuitive, but if you shift some of your time and energy from completing your work to teaching your staff how to do some of it, you will create more time and energy for yourself down the line. Developing your employees' competencies helps you free up your schedule for more important activities (like reevaluating your organization's direction) and allows your staff the opportunity to develop their skills. It's one of your most important and impactful activities, and it's a win–win!

- It should then also make sense that doing the opposite is a losing proposition. Not developing your workers means that you have more to do and the people that work for you lack opportunities to advance. As I saw during my final days at Texas Instruments, people will leave an organization if they aren't given chances to improve their capabilities. Not only that, but you risk impeding your organization's growth too.

There's a useful framework that many of my colleagues and I use to help organizations look for a wider perspective—or, in other words, levitate. It's called the Johari Window model.[3] Maybe you're familiar with it. It's a 2 × 2 matrix that helps with all kinds of organizational roadblocks. There are four cells: what you know, what you don't know, what others know, and what others don't know. Each of these allows a richer

---

[3]J. Luft and H Ingham. 1982. "The Johari Window: A Graphical Model of Awareness in Interpersonal Relations," *NTL Institute.*

understanding of how best to communicate with your organization and uncover mistaken assumptions.

In cell 1, you have what's known by both you and your organization. Everything here is out in the open, ready to be mined for value. Cell 2 has what's known by your organization, but unknown to you, which can represent your blind spots, emerging because of an unintentional ignorance or a withholding of information. In cell 3, you have what's known by you, but unknown to your organization. Here you have an organizational blind spot, where your company is unaware of something internal or external. Finally, in cell 4, you have what's unknown to both you and your organization, where both you and your firm must come together to understand what you as a collective are not seeing (Figure 7.2).

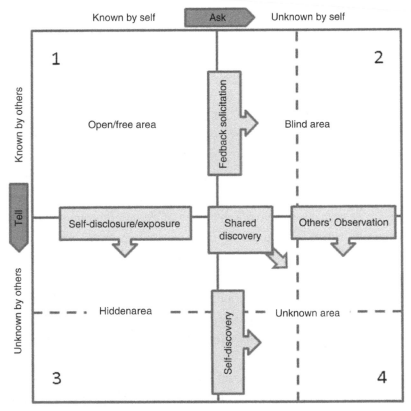

Figure 7.2 Johari window model

When levitating, it's helpful to consider how you can shrink cell 4 as much as possible, which comes back to my point about asking questions in order to map out as much of your internal and external strategies as possible. Consider what you can share with your fellow senior leaders. What about with your board? What can you share with the rest of your organization? Engage with these questions on the meta level.

The most common technique for shrinking your own blind spots is by asking for feedback. What might you ask your staff, partners, peers, or customers that would help uncover some helpful information about yourself? To shrink the blind spots of your organization, what do you need to share with your staff, partners, peers, or customers? How about collaborating to reduce the mutually unknown space? What methods will reveal your collective blind spots? Agile experimentation works perfectly here. Create plans where you don't know the outcome. (Just remember those guardrails!)

Questions like these will never come up in your typical meeting, which is precisely why it's so important you make time to ask them. Good questions represent one of the core values to levitating.

Sometimes, the work required can be quite simple. One of my recent client's company was dealing with a massive change of direction. The President was going from one meeting to another all day, every day. Each day's appointment added to a larger and larger pile of bad news. By the end of every day, not only was he drained, but he was also utterly dispirited and incapable of motivating his team. My advice was to work on actively reengineering his day-to-day experience. I told him to get a breath of fresh air, take a walk, hold one of the meetings outside, or do whatever it took. He needed to figure out how to improve his mental attitude or else the negativity would bog him down and get in the way of any real success.

A straightforward intervention like this can allow us to step back and begin to introduce levitating regularly into our hectic lives. Ross Mason, the founder of the tech company MuleSoft, once shared a telling anecdote in a work session.

Right after his company went public, people began coming up and slyly nudging him, "What are you going to do next?" To which he'd reply, "I'm going to keep looking for ways to add value to MuleSoft." "No, really, what are you going to do?" they'd all ask. But he meant it. He explained that at the end of every year, he'd prop his feet up with a shot glass of whiskey and think about how he could best add value to his company. One year, it might be to focus on technology, the next it might be on his sales force. Whatever area he saw needed attention, he would work on that the following year.

Ross's passion, foresight, and clarity not only took the company to great heights, but it also resulted in a massive buyout from Salesforce—to the tune of $6.5 billion.[4] It seems the hardwork paid off. And what a shining example of levitating!

Of course, more dramatic disruption can warrant very specific and intentional levitating. We experienced this numerous times at Compaq.

For many years, computer companies sold through distributors. They'd design and manufacture the product and sell them in bulk to vendors, who would offer them directly to consumers. Some of you might remember ComputerLand, one of the widespread retailers. In those days, the average consumer knew very little about how computers worked or which one was the best for their needs. And yet at the same time, the capabilities this machine offered made it an asset to both individuals and businesses. This dynamic created the need for a middleman to guide consumers through the process of buying a personal computer.

However, there came the point when the market shifted. Consumers suddenly felt comfortable buying their computers directly from the manufacturers. It turned Compaq's business model on its head. Companies with which we had partnered, like ComputerLand, had the rug pulled out from under them. All of their business disappeared. To survive, Compaq had to respond quickly and effectively. We had to shift our operations from serving retailers to serving consumers, which required stepping back from the situation—or levitating—to recognize the shift in the market and understand that our loyal customers were about to go out of business. At the business model level, this is a shift from a B2B model to a B2C (Business to Business vs. Business to Consumer)

---

[4]J. Novet. April 3, 2018. "Salesforce reveals it was the sole bidder for MuleSoft and even paid 18 percent more than its original offer," *CNBC.*

Another example of levitating came after I left Compaq. I had spent 14 years pouring myself into a company that had skyrocketed in size and revenue. Suddenly, I was on my own.

And I had no idea what I was going to do. When I'd tell people this, they would exclaim, "What do you mean you don't know what you're going to do?" The truth was, not only did I not know what I wanted to do, I didn't *want* to know! I understood at the time that there were so many unexplored possibilities I needed to experience before I could commit to a particular path. I was able to see, on a meta level, that it wasn't time to take the next step yet. First, I had to survey my options.

Another long-time client of mine has sought outlets for meta-level foresight. His name is Dave Keil, and he's the CEO of the Inc. 500 software testing company QASymphony. I had the pleasure to sit down with him and discuss the behaviors and communities he's found to be the most helpful with his levitating.

Endeavor, a global nonprofit organization that seeks to help entrepreneurs maximize their potential and grow the entrepreneurial communities around the world, has been an incredibly fruitful resource for Dave. The executive retreat they host has put him in touch with a diverse set of minds. He was able to discover new frameworks for facing challenges and opportunities as an audience member, while sharing his own two cents and collaborating on new ideas as an active participant.

> The CEOs can come together and learn from other established CEOs that have already scaled their firms. I've found those sessions during the past couple of years to be outstanding for getting a different viewpoint and taking the blinders off. I can't say enough about that network. It's not only successful from a vertical standpoint, but it's also been very effective from a global perspective. To get the perspective of CEOs from Brazil, Morocco, and other countries to which I would normally not be exposed has been extremely valuable. I have had the opportunity—to see how they think about business and to learn how they tackle their challenges.

The same has been true about Insight IGNITE Innovation Roundtable series, another offsite event that brings together executives to shed light on cutting-edge topics in the tech industry as well as to connect leaders from all kinds of different backgrounds.

They focus on bringing together very established Chief Information Officers (CIOs) from global organizations. I just attended this event for three-and-a-half days in Iceland, and the level of executives and outside speakers at this event was exceptional. Regarding topics of conversation—it was everything from artificial intelligence to digital transformation to scaling organizations to talking about catalysts for being bolder. It added value to what had traditionally been a gap.

But how about your senior team? How can you bring this kind of value back from a retreat? How else might an organization's executives inject this meta zone thinking into their workday?

It's so easy to get bogged down in the day-to-day. I see through my experiences how valuable it is to have these different perspectives—whether it's outside training or interaction with some of the teams at Insight. We have a few board advisory members, and they've been very impactful. I've highly encouraged bringing in or working with third parties, including mentors and coaches, who can offer a different viewpoint to the senior team.

It comes back to interfering with your typical thought process to change the channel and think about things in a new way. How might you rewire your schemas, adopt a refreshing new framework, or challenge your team to problem solve in a new way? Once you can break away from autopilot and begin to see things through a fresh lens, you can levitate.

The last piece here will be to integrate this into your organization's operations. It must be a continual practice. Otherwise, how valuable can any of this be? Successfully adding levitating to your behavior involves diligence, consistency, and commitment.

Make It Real

It's time to take some notes. What would it look like for you to levitate? How about you and your senior team? What kind of timeframe could you arrange for yourself and your team? What environment changes or other techniques might help you disconnect from distractions of narrow ways of thinking? What disruptions might be worth exploring? Are there any major disruptions you feel like you or your organization is ignoring? Which ones might be too pivotal to keep ignoring? What kind of questions are you looking into? Are there any major disruptions you feel like you or your organization are ignoring? Which ones might be too pivotal to keep ignoring? What kind of questions never get raised at a meeting? What do you wish you could ask your staff, peers, or CEO that you've never gotten the chance to ask?

_____

_____

_____

_____

_____

_____

_____

_____

SECTION 3

Avoiding the "So What"

CHAPTER 8

Nourishing Your Cell

Putting It All Together

Our philosophy is that we care about people first.

—Mark Zuckerberg

Remember back in high school when your science teacher explained how cells are made of molecules, and how they are made of atoms? We all got the lesson at one point or another: life is complex and relies on systems within systems to function. You need the right kind of atoms *and* the right kind of molecules to make up a healthy cell.

Each system has its characteristics, its governing laws, and its functions—all the while fitting within the larger framework it occupies. You can choose to look at this as separate systems working within their confines or as separate systems working together. I prefer to view them as interdependent. And you should, too (Figure 8.1).

This multisystem hierarchy is an analogy for the different pieces that make up every business. Replace the cell with the organization, the molecules with the teams, and the atoms with the individuals. For the cell to be complete and healthy, it has to have the necessary molecules and atoms, which also have to be sound in their own right. In the same

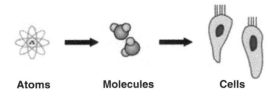

Atoms   Molecules   Cells

Figure 8.1 Atoms, molecules, and cells

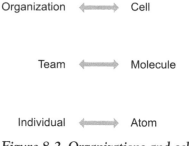

Figure 8.2 Organizations and cells

manner, you keep your business whole by ensuring that your teams are successful and you guarantee that your teams are successful by making sure that each individual is high performing. It's a straightforward concept, and yet so many people struggle to determine that each rung of the hierarchy is functioning at its best (Figure 8.2).

The core of this chapter is the *collective implementation* of all five of the strategies I've defined. I find this biological framework a metaphor for understanding how the strategies must be integrated and executed not just with senior executives, but at every level of your organization.

Putting all of these strategies together is as much a question of *who* as it is a question of *how.* Atoms must have the right kind of charge, molecules must be properly bonded, and cells must have functioning organelles. Similarly, individuals must be high performing and clear headed, teams must be collaborative and communicative, and an organization must be continually strategizing and looking toward the future. And, just like in biology, for one rung of the hierarchy to be successfully functioning, the one below it must be as well. An organization is as good as its teams and a team is only as capable as the participating members, including its leaders.

Deciding to see your business through these three different groupings allows you to create significant change. This bottom–up perspective will reinforce the values of my five strategies on a granular level. Your goal here should be to weave the philosophies that underpin these strategies into the fabric of your culture. You want it to be the air people breathe.

Using this framework to view the system is ultimately how these five strategies become sustainable. Some businesses—like Compaq—begin with these values. Others have to feed them retroactively into the culture of their organization.

If you find your organization falls into the second category, I want to emphasize that implementing these systemic changes is a process, so it's important not to get too focused on immediate results. In many cases, you're asking your workforce to reconfigure schemas of how to behave and do their job. That's not something to take lightly.

Consider the Kübler–Ross change curve as a way to map this internal disruption.[1] As you strategize with individuals, teams, and your organization as a whole, you should pay careful attention to how workers are experiencing the change. Where in the process of integration are people getting stuck? This question will be essential for dealing with the mental roadblocks that you, your team, or your workers will face (Figure 8.3).

I'd urge you to take this a step further and explicitly introduce the change curve as part of implementing the strategies. If you can make conscious the process of accepting what is new and foreign, you will see your organization accelerate even more. You, your team, and your workers should be *learning how to learn.*

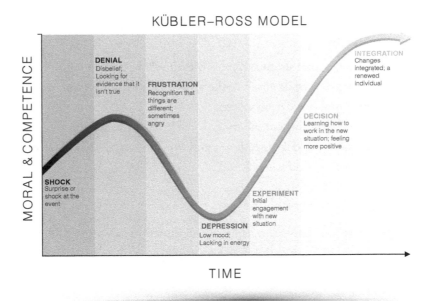

Figure 8.3 *Kübler–Ross change curve*

---

[1]"Understanding the Kubler–Ross Change Curve," *Cleverism*, March 12, 2016.

A useful starting point for helping those going through the change is to first explore what it might look like to operate differently. Often we've worked similarly in the past, but not with the required discipline or consistency. Try to nudge particular processes into place until they become routine.

Each level of your cell will need to be taken care of and managed in different ways. Just like a cell relies on molecules to exist, so do molecules rely on atoms. But the three groupings don't all have the same needs. The makeup and functionality of a cell are radically different than the makeup of a molecule or atom.

By the same logic, an organization has different qualities than a team, and a team has different characteristics from an individual. Here's a more explicit outline of how to support each level.

Nourishing Your Cell

1. Every individual should . . .

- Have the information and support he (or she) need to do his (or her) job.
- Feel the freedom to accomplish required tasks in the most fulfilling way, while ensuring the responsibilities are helpful to the organization's overall success.
- Understand his contribution to the organization as a whole. It should be evident to him *why* and *how* he is an essential piece of the puzzle, and where he fits.

2. Every team should . . .

- Have different requirements and supervision—some will be high performing and not demand any guidance, while others will be dumbed down and require attention.
- Evaluate its effectiveness as a unit. Some will do better functioning as a collaborative group, rather than a cohesive team. Likewise, some groups will do better functioning as a tight team.
- Understand and operate with cross-functional skills and relationships.

3. Every organization should . . .

- Have a corporate calendar to outline significant dates. Explicit intentions must be set on measuring success, evaluating and reevaluating strategy, responding to internal and external disruption, and thinking in the meta zone.
- Emphasize on development of internal and external strategy. Always be looking ahead to how you can innovate to garner more internal operational success and create better rewards for everyone involved.
- Be value driven. Is every member spending his time efficiently? Is anyone's potential being dumbed down? What can be done to create higher value for you, your staff, your partners, and your customers?
- Be open to rescheduling, but not canceling, when urgent issues arise. Formulating and addressing strategy will always take precedent over other work. There must be a commitment to accomplish these kinds of goals.

You may be asking yourself how this all differ from the last chapter on levitating. While operating at the meta level is similar, there's a difference. Nourishing your cell means getting into a rhythm, so these strategies become habitual. It means internalizing what success looks like for your organization and having a workforce that knows how their jobs tie back to the vision of your business.

Levitating allows you and your team to survey the big picture—but that's still an intentional exercise. This chapter is about taking all of my strategies, which address both the macro and micro, and ingraining them in your organization's subconscious.

But I don't want this to turn into every other business book and begin prescribing all these arbitrary parameters. There is no formula for getting all of this exactly right. Every business has different circumstances. My approach has always been to use what works for your company as long as you schedule meetings in advance and people are prepared to discuss what's important.

I'll also add that *explicit* and *meaningful* communication goes a long way. It's hard enough to convey old ideas, never mind new ones. Just because you commented, sent out a memo, or gave a PowerPoint presentation does not mean that you've successfully communicated.

And it doesn't just come down to repetition. Those who are receiving your message will need to understand it in the way that's most useful to them. No matter what role he or she plays, every worker with whom you're communicating will approach the discussion with the same question, "What does this mean for me?" It will be your job to answer this honestly. Some will need to understand the logic behind the information, while others will need to know the emotion behind it. Some will be looking for the big picture interpretation. Others will need a detailed play-by-play explanation. Every worker should be able to walk away knowing exactly how this new information is going to affect him or her.

Sometimes, communication is just a forgotten first step. I had a client once who was running into a lot of difficulty with a merger and needed help getting started on the transition. The management came to me for advice on a rollout plan. I told them before you focus on the merger itself, you need a communications plan. How else is everyone going to know what's happening and why? Or, more importantly, what does it mean to your employees and what do they need to do to ensure success?

Last, but not the least, I also recommend a quarterly off-site retreat for you and your senior team. All of my most successful clients have made this nonnegotiable protocol. Other than that, here are some general techniques I've seen work wonders with businesses trying to implement my strategies collectively.

The Cell

It's a good idea for you or your team to find a mentor, someone who knows what success looks like in your space, especially given the resources with which you have to work.

Some companies hire consultants, some have informal advisers, and others have official advisory boards. The benefit to having a third party like this in the room comes from the objective party's ability to keep people in check and accountable. A third party also has the opportunity to model behavior and strategy—some people even shadow you on the job. There's real value in having someone in the room watch your performance and draw a comparison to your potential.

When I attend meetings, it's often as a facilitator to help drive productivity and constructive dialogue. We get super broad *and* super specific: we cover everything from high-level strategy to extremely minute issues. When people isolate conversation to one department, I always bring it back to cross-functionality. I want the understanding of the group to be focused, yet holistic.

I also have frequent correspondence with the senior team, offering feedback and doing check-ins. I'm less a referee and more of a coach. While my presence allows the team to explore new ideas safely and intelligently, the eventual hope is that the senior team learns these skills themselves. As a consultant, I measure success by my ability to walk away and see the organization continuing with their high-performing behavior without needing my help.

The Molecules

If this already reflects how your organization's senior executives operate, you should take a look at how you treat your teams. One technique I've seen work with past clients has been to initiate talent reviews.

You bring in the central teams that make up your organization and take a look at their performance. Are the team members all functioning at their highest potential? Is anything dumbing down the team's success? The structure of these evaluations can vary quite a bit.

One tactic is to bring awareness to individual strengths and weaknesses to better diagnose what the team needs. There may be untapped potential from a specific employee that could accelerate a team's success if only he received the right attention. The same can apply to someone who's impeding progress. As you're about to see, this kind of granule evaluation can come in handy.

The Atoms

Talent reviews are a fantastic tool for evaluating individual workers. An explicit structure for this kind of process is a great way to define what your goals, expectations, and concerns are with your employees. Reviews let them know exactly into what they should be investing the most time, energy, and thought.

Here are a few great questions every worker should be able to answer in the process.

- How do I contribute to my organization and why is that valuable?
- What strengths do I have?
- What areas of my performance do I need to develop?

If a worker has specific areas he or she needs to improve, an organized process for the evaluation should help identify specific strategies to grow. Every individual should walk away feeling supported.

I think it's most fruitful to give your staff as much feedback as you can. And the more immediate, the better. If you follow up with informal feedback daily or weekly, your employees will more likely develop habits aligned with your expectations. Add onto that a quarterly meeting to ensure everyone is still working toward their goals, and you should begin to see results. A more formal talent review can be scheduled once or twice a year.

Finally, give each worker the opportunity to have his or her voice heard. Ask for feedback on your behavior. What are you doing that's working or isn't working? Is there anything about which your employees routinely complain? What are you doing right that you should be increasing?

Next, ask workers what their plans are, and how your organization might be able to help them. Remember, your organization is only as good as the sum of its parts. Caring for your employees is a legitimate investment in your success. Your concern lets your workers know your organization is interested in them and their ability to grow, which will improve loyalty and decrease turnover. Caring about employees is valuable to any business that wants to retain its institutional knowledge, rather than wasting resources educating new workers on the same systems of operation.

Let's take a look at a quintessential example: a company that started with a singular vision, but has since engineered success on a variety of fronts—both by dominating established industries and reinventing others. Not only is the company a household name, but it probably knows more about your home-life than you'd like: Facebook.

Love or hate them; this is a company that has benefited from nourishing its cell. On an organizational level, it has kept its gaze facing forward, setting the standard for a successful and monetizable social network. Acquiring potential competition like Instagram and WhatsApp, its reach continues to expand and bleed into neighboring markets. As of 2018, there are 2.1 billion users out of the 4 billion that have access to the Internet.[2]

In 2008, Mark Zuckerberg hired Sheryl Sandberg as the company's COO. It was a smart move forward because of Sandberg's ability to excel where Zuckerberg fell flat. One of her first projects was building Facebook's desktop's interface to better support the company's potential as a highly personalized data-fueled ad platform. However, by 2012, the climbing number of mobile users had become a legitimate threat to their desktop-centered business model. It was an exemplary moment to react with agility, and within 3 years, the company had successfully integrated mobile ads into the Facebook app.[3]

But the real takeaway here comes from the company's numbers. In 2015, Facebook made nearly eight times as much from mobile ads as Twitter and is projected to make almost 15 times as much in 2018.[4] On one hand, we should account for Facebook's sheer reach compared with Twitter's (there are approximately six Facebook users for every one Twitter user).[5,6] But on the other hand, it's worth noting the dif-

---

[2]S. Kemp. January 30, 2018. "Digital in 2018: World's Internet Users Pass the 4 Billion Mark," *We are Social.*

[3]"The new face of Facebook: How to win friends and influence people," *The Economist,* April 9, 2016.

[4]"Mobile internet advertising revenues of major ad-selling companies worldwide from 2015 to 2018 (in billion U.S. dollars)," *eMarketer,* October, 2016.

[5]"Number of monthly active Twitter users worldwide from 1st quarter 2010 to 4th quarter 2017 (in millions)," *Statista,* 2018.

[6]"Number of monthly active Facebook users worldwide as of 4th quarter 2017 (in millions)," *Statista,* 2018.

MOBILE AD REVENUES OF FACEBOOK AND TWITTER WORLDWIDE, 2015–2018 (IN BILLION U.S. DOLLARS)

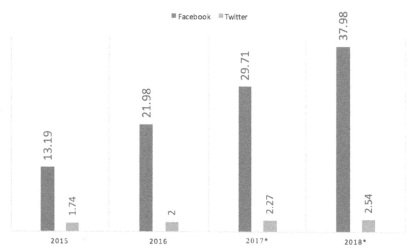

Figure 8.4 Mobile Ad revenues of Facebook and Twitter

ferences in management between the two companies. Around that same time in 2015, Twitter was consistently dealing with turnover of their top-level executives, a struggle that has continued until today (Figure 8.4).[7]

This difference in stable leadership may not be the root of the two companies' varying success, but I can't imagine how productivity can soar in an environment where bosses are moving through a revolving door every year. Not only does stable leadership ensure less wasted time to relearn the same protocol, but it also creates insulation. It allows the organization's culture to begin operating with cohesion and systemically embody a singular vision.

What's more, Zuckerberg nourishes his teams and the individuals that comprise them. Out of all the top Silicon Valley tech giants, Facebook has

---

[7]J. Dunn. September 28, 2016. "Look at how many executives have left Twitter over the years," *Business Insider.*

the highest employee retention rate.[8] Not to mention the fact that the company has been rated several times as the best place to work in the United States.[9]

Zuckerberg is not only driving his company to greater heights, but by nourishing the cell, he's also taking care of his molecules and atoms. Caitlin Kalinowski, Facebook's product design engineering director, summed it up nicely when explaining to *Business Insider* how the company hired her.

> Mark Zuckerberg ended up calling me, which was unexpected. I think that's one of the things that's impressive about him in particular. I feel like he reaches down deep into his organizations—in recruiting, but also in getting to know people.[10]

Now picture your business. Hold it up to Facebook and see how it compares. Are there any glaringly obvious faults? Or do you feel like you're embodying most or all of these strategies? I'm sure you can answer for you and your senior team, but what would lower level staff say? How about those entry-level workers that have just come on board? If you had to grade how managers nourish each level of your organization, what grades would you give out?

To take some of the stress out of this, I've put together a template that can help with compartmentalizing some of the primary variables.

This template is by no means exhaustive, but it's a great place to start. Take a look (Figure 8.5).

---

[8] B. Peterson, "Travis Kalanick lasted in his role for 6.5 years—five times longer than the average Uber employee," *Business Insider,* August 20, 2017.

[9] R. Gillett. December 7, 2017. "7 reasons Facebook is the best place to work in America and no other company can compare," *Business Insider.*

[10] A. Cain. December 7, 2017. "What it's REALLY like to work at Facebook," *Business Insider.*

THE BIG FIVE
No-nonsense Strategies for Internal and External Alignment

	Red Flags	Next Steps	So What?
No Dumbing Down	• Poor interpersonal skills • Cynicism • Misaligned goals and priorities • Weak leadership • No consequences for poor performance	• Value process and content • Ask for what you want, notice what you get • Pay attention! • Get the skills • Walk the talk	• Include a formal debrief on content and process in our major meetings. • Use a 9-box review for talent annually and take developmental actions
Doubling Back	• Mired in process • Can't repeat, can't scale, etc. • Overvaluing processes, tools, documentation, contracts, plans, etc.	• Identify your coordinates • Decide on goals • Examine doubling back functionally and cross-functionally • Execute plan and track progress	• Invest in lead generation this year • Schedule informal time with employees and customers • Review process scalability with each SVP
Playing Bumper Cars	• Slow or stagnant growth • Strategies and tactics feel irrelevant, archaic • What you planned for was not what you got	• Define your goals • Put guardrails in place • Execute and monitor • Adjust and redraw guardrails as circumstances change	• Ask staff what they perceive as "sacred cows" • Shut down Product X that doesn't solve true pain points • Pivot Product Y based on feedback from
Becoming a Utility	• Inefficient processes • Rigidity, extreme resistance to change • Difficult to replicate successes • Hard to scale	• Create thresholds • Prioritize impact • Redesign processes • Hire and reward the behaviors and skills that you need	• Hire Top notch finance leader and A+ team • Create real time accounting so we can focus on future planning • Focus on channel partners as key
Learning to Levitate	• Bogged down by the day to day • Blindspots • Missed opportunities • Lots of FOMO	• Create time to think • Ask questions • Say no to shiny new objects • Develop your employees • Ask for feedback and solicit different POVs • Debrief and learn	• Seek out and actively participate in P.E. networking • Schedule time with peers who have successfully scaled • Develop advisory board to expose staff to senior third parties

Figure 8.5 Template of five no-nonsense strategies

CHAPTER 9

How to Begin

The First Step to Success

It always seems impossible until it's done.

—Nelson Mandela

There isn't much more I can tell you here except to go out and start working.

You've got all the strategies, you know how to implement them at each level of your organization, and you understand that, rather than just introducing new protocol, you need to change the way you and your workers think. The only question you might be asking yourself is, "Where do I start?"

Like Every Significant Undertaking, the Key Is to Start Small and Commit

The last thing you want to do is to announce an overambitious game plan, inspire your staff, and then dash their hopes when your organization bites off more than it can chew. Not only will you disappoint your employees, but they'll also lose faith in you as a driver of change.

You should begin by outlining your first step and by selecting the "low-hanging fruit." Set a couple of different goals for challenges or opportunities you know are within your organization's reach. Next, pick one long-term goal. This goal-setting will ensure that you're garnering momentum and making progress, but not just subsisting on the adrenaline rush of being productive in the short term.

Once your company starts making substantial progress with these first couple of commitments, you can begin to add more to your plate.

Be sure to stay consistent with those high-level discussions, too, so you can continue to keep your internal and external strategies aligned.

The speaker and writer Simon Sinek offers a pertinent nugget of advice here. It's a critical insight on why modern business practices are particularly unbalanced, and what can be done to correct the situation. His advice distinguishes *intensity* from *consistency*.[1] He explains that modern business practices praise working fast and hard to ensure you see results as quickly as possible. In other words, there's a massive amount of value assigned to intensity. But while it's true that an enthusiastic and determined work ethic is a step in the right direction, you can't have lasting or sustainable impact simply through intensity. You also need *consistency*.

Sinek puts it quite elegantly, "You can't get into shape by going to the gym for 9 hours. It won't work. But if you work out every single day for 20 minutes, you will absolutely get into shape." You have to ensure you're working on your goals consistently, not only intensely. It may be less exciting, but if you treat your work as an investment in your organization's future, it'll be easier to stay disciplined.

A frustrating example of this comes up in many sales organizations. Each year, the senior sales leader brings in a new trainer with a novel methodology to teach the same sales force. The trainer puts on an exciting little seminar and the staff walk away feeling energized, and maybe they even try some of their newly learned skills. But within a few weeks, everyone is back to functioning like they had in the past.

The problem? It's all just intensity! There's no emphasis put on consistency. The real breakthroughs will happen when you can get your sales force to concentrate on developing a small set of skills. You will see much better results if you can get your teams *really* good at one or two methodologies, rather than stay mediocre with five or six.

Set Your Goals and Free Up Resources by Prioritizing

We all have an overflowing list of "to-dos," and it's hard to know which deserve your attention now rather than later. Maybe you have several

---

[1]Z. Thompson. September 22, 2017. "Let's Talk About the Difference Between Intensity and Consistency," *Huffington Post*.

short-term goals that are easy to attain, but they're not core components of your success. Or perhaps you need to be spending much more time working toward that long-term agenda item.

Here's the Eisenhower Matrix, a straightforward 2 × 2 matrix to help mitigate some of the stress that emerges from prioritizing. It was designed by the one and only Dwight Eisenhower to help craft a hyper-productive life. In addition to being the 34th president of the United States, he worked in a variety of other top-tier political positions, served in high-ranking military roles, and even was able to pursue oil painting, aided by this framework.

All you need to do is ask yourself: is the task at hand important or unimportant, and urgent or not urgent? Asking yourself these questions will allow you to decide exactly what kind of action is required and when: now or later (Figure 9.1).

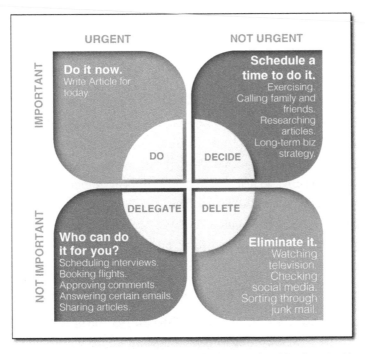

"What is important is seldom urgent and what is urgent is seldom important."
—**Dwight Eisenhower, 34th President of the United States**

Figure 9.1 The Eisenhower box

Source: https://jamesclear.com/eisenhower-box

If you're dealing with an agenda item that's urgent and important, it should make sense that it demands your immediate attention. You may convene a meeting with your team to address next steps and outline a game plan as soon as possible. Whereas if it's important but not urgent, you should find a useful way to create time in your schedule, acknowledging that it must be dealt with effectively, just not at this time. These will be agenda items that are not time-sensitive, so you can take your time making thoughtful and strategic decisions about how to move forward.

If a to-do arises that is urgent but unimportant, it is worth delegating. Is there a specific team, department, or lower-level staff member who can take care of this for you? These tasks may require supervision, but it will be in your interest if you can devote your attention to other more pressing issues. Finally, an agenda item that is unimportant and not urgent should be eliminated. If there's a task that's not serving you and it's taking up lots of your time, you may need to walk away from it.

Prioritizing is a useful tool if you've outlined several low-hanging fruit, but don't know which ones to go after first. Consider using this matrix as a launch pad for more in-depth discussion about the payoffs of various trajectories and how you would like to divide responsibilities.

The matrix can also help you to shift your focus from immediate goals to long-term objectives. Tasks that fall into the "important and not urgent" box can serve as an entry point to levitating and discussing your organization's broader agenda—in other words, operating in the meta zone.

Stay Accountable

No matter what the scale or impact of the project you're taking on, you want to ensure follow through. Your follow-up can be done on an individual level or cross-organizationally.

Many of my clients come to me in dire need of course correction—but sometimes all that means is holding people to their word. As a consultant, this is one of my functions. It can be as simple as a weekly call with a COO to check up on operations. What matters is that those drivers of change feel personally responsible for their actions.

Those who are closer to the ground level should also feel personally responsible. By this, I mean your workers should understand their impact. A great way to grow accountability within your workforce is to shift the focus from the results you're getting to the process by which you're getting them. Emphasizing on the *how* of success will allow staff to feel valued and needed.

Focusing on the *how* will also help you identify what is working and what isn't. It's great to praise your team for closing a large deal, but it's even more fruitful to recognize the processes that got you to that contract so you're able to recreate the same success next time—or, better yet, so you're able to seal an even larger one next time.

This kind of shift in behavior can have a profound impact on your organization's growth. It's also a great reason to debrief regularly, whether with your senior team or your staff. You can ensure accountability from others. In the same way, I ensure accountability from my clients.

Feeling unsure about how accountable you and your organization are? Take a look at another 2 × 2 matrix. This matrix is one I devised to help my clients understand the harm that comes from working with unaccountable people and the accelerated success that can come from working with those who are highly accountable (Figure 9.2).

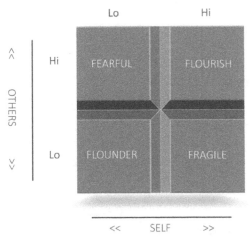

Figure 9.2 Four quadrants of accountability

If you find that you and your team are unreliable, your organization will flounder, as no productivity is guaranteed. If you hold yourself accountable, while your colleagues don't, you'll find yourself in a fragile position because your output will be promised while their results will not.

However, if your team is accountable but you aren't, you'll be fearful, struggling to please those with whom you work. And finally—the quadrant everyone should strive to embody—if both you and your colleagues are being held accountable, then the odds are increased that you will all flourish because of the added support for your team to meet its goals.

But remember, how are you to expect your fellow leaders and staff to put in the work to rewire their behavior and create new habits, if you won't?

Marshall Goldsmith's and Mark Reiter's book, *Triggers: Creating Behavior That Lasts—Becoming the Person You Want to Be*, gives a detailed account of what informs both conscious and unconscious behavior and offers techniques to reengineer this behavior actively.[2] There is a lot of research out there about how our brains and bodies work to reinforce patterns and dismantle others. Like I've said before, the kind of change I've discussed throughout this book depends significantly on your ability to change your schemas and skills.

Remind Yourself Who's Holding the Reins Here

As a senior leader, you and your team wield the most power in your organization (or, possess the most responsibility). When compared with any other group or position in your business, you have the most influence and the best chance of success.

Your ability to lead is both a privilege and responsibility—there's no one else who's going to remind you to stay agile, function like a utility, or operate in the meta zone.

---

[2]M. Goldsmith and M. Reiter. 2015. *Triggers: Creating Behavior That Lasts—Becoming the Person You Want to Be* (New York: Crown Business).

If disruption is wreaking havoc on your organization, your team is the last line of defense. If there's a brilliant opportunity waiting for you to leverage, your team must be the one that takes-and-leads action.

If you read this whole book and had your interest piqued by a few interesting concepts, don't nod your head and go back to business as usual. Pull out that legal pad or open up that mind mapping app, and begin brainstorming how you're going to get the attention of your senior team. Schedule a meeting right now. Make that call. Many organizations have already started applying these strategies and have seen enormous success. Not addressing internal and external misalignments puts your organization at a severe disadvantage, which may or may not be fatal.

But if you *are* ready, if you feel equipped, and want to dive headfirst into radical organizational change, you should have everything you need in your toolkit.

These five strategies were not selected because they're simple or easy to explain. I chose them because they've been the most useful and accessible to organizations of all kinds in a variety of different industries. I decided they were worth synthesizing into a book because I've seen them get the best results.

The final ingredient here should be obvious—a willingness to try, to fail, to get back up, and do better. I joined Compaq in my mid-20s; I had nothing to lose and everything to gain. But Rod Canion, Jim Harris, and Bill Murto? They had families and careers. They walked away from senior management positions in other well-established firms to leap into work that required every last bit of their time and energy.

It wasn't just a matter of strategy. Launching Compaq took a significant dose of ingenuity, resourcefulness, and aligned intentions. But before all that, it required bravery and a decision to challenge the status quo. So ask yourself, did you pick up this book out of fear? What might you accomplish if you instead operate from a place of courage and conviction? Rather than settling for what you know, what if you venture to explore what's possible?

About the Author

Karen Walker is a consultant and advisor to CEOs and senior organization leaders in many fields of industry. She helps her clients grow their companies with successful outcomes that include IPOs, acquisitions, market share increases, and significant leadership development. She has advised dozens of companies, from start-ups to nonprofits to Fortune 500 firms, including Aetna and BMC Software.

Prior to launching her consultancy, Karen spent 14 years in leadership roles at Compaq Computer, then the fastest growing company in American history. As VP of Operating Services for Global Infrastructure, she helped spur the creation of more than $15 billion in value.

Karen has a BS in engineering from Texas A&M University and graduated from the ODHRM Program at Columbia University. She has served on advisory committees to Rice University and Texas A&M University and on the executive board of The Alley Theatre in Houston. She currently resides in Jupiter, Florida, although she can most often be found aloft in seat 2C.

Index

OTHER TITLES IN THE HUMAN RESOURCE MANAGEMENT AND ORGANIZATIONAL BEHAVIOR COLLECTION

- *Creating a Successful Consulting Practice* by Gary W. Randazzo
- *How Successful Engineers Become Great Business Leaders* by Paul Rulkens
- *Leading the High-Performing Company: A Transformational Guide to Growing Your Business and Outperforming Your Competition* by Heidi Pozzo
- *The Concise Coaching Handbook: How to Coach Yourself and Others to Get Business Results* by Elizabeth Dickinson
- *Lead Self First Before Leading Others: A Life Planning Resource* by Stephen K. Hacker
- *The How of Leadership: Inspire People to Achieve Extraordinary Results* by Maxwell Ubah
- *Managing Organizational Change: The Measurable Benefits of Applied iOCM* by Linda C. Mattingly
- *Creating the Accountability Culture: The Science of Life Changing Leadership* by Yvonnne Thompson
- *Conflict and Leadership: How to Harness the Power of Conflict to Create Better Leaders and Build Thriving Teams* by Christian Muntean
- *Precision Recruitment Skills: How to Find the Right Person For the Right Job, the First Time* by Rod Matthews
- *Practical Performance Improvement: How to Be an Exceptional People Manager* by Rod Matthews
- *Creating Leadership: How to Change Hippos Into Gazelles* by Philip Goodwin and Tony Page
- *Uncovering the Psychology of Good Bosses vs Bad Bosses and What it Means for Leaders: How to Avoid the High Cost of Bad Leadership* by Debra Dupree
- *Competency Based Education: How to Prepare College Graduates for the World of Work* by Nina Morel and Bruce Griffiths

Announcing the Business Expert Press Digital Library

Concise e-books business students need for classroom and research

This book can also be purchased in an e-book collection by your library as

- *a one-time purchase,*
- *that is owned forever,*
- *allows for simultaneous readers,*
- *has no restrictions on printing, and*
- *can be downloaded as PDFs from within the library community.*

Our digital library collections are a great solution to beat the rising cost of textbooks. E-books can be loaded into their course management systems or onto students' e-book readers. The **Business Expert Press** digital libraries are very affordable, with no obligation to buy in future years. For more information, please visit **www.businessexpertpress.com/librarians**. To set up a trial in the United States, please email **sales@businessexpertpress.com**.

CPSIA information can be obtained
at www.ICGtesting.com
Printed in the USA
LVHW09s0343251018
594771LV00016B/641/P

9 781947 441804